Service User and Carer Participation in Social Work

Transforming Social Work Practice – titles in the series

Applied Psychology for Social Work	ISBN-13 978 1 84445 071 8
Collaborative Social Work Practice	ISBN-13 978 1 84445 014 5
Communication and Interpersonal Skills in Social Work	ISBN-13 978 1 84445 019 0
Courtroom Skills for Social Workers	ISBN-13 978 1 84445 123 4
Effective Practice Learning in Social Work	ISBN-13 978 1 84445 015 2
Groupwork Practice in Social Work	ISBN-13 978 1 84445 086 2
Loss and Social Work	ISBN-13 978 1 84445 088 6
Management and Organisations in Social Work	ISBN-13 978 1 84445 044 2
New Directions in Social Work	ISBN-13 978 1 84445 079 4
Practical Computer Skills for Social Work	ISBN-13 978 1 84445 031 2
Reflective Practice in Social Work	ISBN-13 978 1 84445 082 4
Service User and Carer Participation in Social Work	ISBN-13 978 1 84445 074 9
Sexuality and Social Work	ISBN-13 978 1 84445 085 5
Social Work and Human Development (second edition)	ISBN-13 978 1 84445 112 8
Social Work and Mental Health (third edition)	ISBN-13 978 1 84445 154 8
Social Work in Education and Children's Services	ISBN-13 978 1 84445 045 9
Social Work Practice: Assessment, Planning, Intervention and Review (second edition)	ISBN-13 978 1 84445 113 5
Social Work with Children and Families (second edition)	ISBN-13 978 1 84445 144 9
Social Work with Children, Young People and their Families in Scotland (second edition)	ISBN-13 978 1 84445 156 2
Social Work with Drug and Substance Misusers	ISBN-13 978 1 84445 058 9
Social Work with Looked After Children	ISBN-13 978 1 84445 103 6
Social Work with Older People (second edition)	ISBN-13 978 1 84445 155 5
Social Work with People with Learning Difficulties	ISBN-13 978 1 84445 042 8
Sociology and Social Work	ISBN-13 978 1 84445 087 9
Studying for Your Social Work Degree	ISBN-13 978 1 84445 174 6
Thriving and Surviving in Social Work	ISBN-13 978 1 84445 080 0
Using the Law in Social Work (third edition)	ISBN-13 978 1 84445 114 2
Values and Ethics in Social Work	ISBN-13 978 1 84445 067 1
What is Social Work? Context and Perspectives (second edition)	ISBN- 978 1 84445 055 1
Youth Justice and Social Work	ISBN- 978 1 84445 066 4

To order, please contact our distributor: BEBC Distribution, Albion Close, Parkstone, Poole, BH12 3LL. Telephone: 0845 230 9000, email: learningmatters@bebc.co.uk. You can also find more information on each of these titles and our other learning resources at www.learningmatters.co.uk.

Service User and Carer Participation in Social Work

JANET WARREN

Series Editors: Jonathan Parker and Greta Bradley

LearningMatters

First published in 2007 by Learning Matters Ltd
Reprinted in 2008

British Library Cataloguing in Publication Data
A CIP record for this book is available from the British Library

ISBN 978 1 84445 074 9

Cover and text design by Code 5
Project Management by Deer Park Productions, Tavistock, Devon
Typeset by Pantek Arts Ltd, Maidstone, Kent
Printed and bound in Great Britain by Cromwell Press Ltd, Trowbridge, Wiltshire

Learning Matters Ltd
33 Southernhay East
Exeter EX1 1NX
Tel: 01392 215560
info@learningmatters.co.uk
www.learningmatters.co.uk

Contents

Acknowledgements   vii

Introduction   ix

1   Understanding service user and carer involvement and participation   1

2   Origins and development of service user and carer involvement and participation   30

3   Service user and carer involvement and participation: rhetoric or reality?   46

4   Empowering service user and carer participation   61

5   Participation in practice: involving adults   79

6   Participation in practice: involving children   97

Conclusion   117

Appendix   119

References   127

Index   139

Acknowledgements

Sincere thanks are due to the many service users, carers, practitioners, students and higher education teams who, over the years, have nurtured and helped to develop my own knowledge and understanding of service user and carer involvement and participation in social work practice. I would also like to thank all the individuals and organisations who have offered advice and support in the drafting of this work. I hope very much that its contents reflect the richness of their knowledge and experience.

I must also extend thanks to my family whose patience and support have made this book possible.

Acknowledgements

Introduction

This book is written for student social workers who are beginning to develop their skills and understanding of the requirements for practice, specifically with regard to the involvement and participation of service users and carers. Whilst it is primarily aimed at students in their first year or level of study, it will be useful for subsequent years depending on how your programme is arranged, what you are studying and especially as you move into practice learning. The book will also appeal to people who are considering a career in social work or social care, but not yet studying for a social work degree. It will assist students undertaking a range of health and social care courses in further education by providing them with an understanding of some of the ways in which social workers practise. Nurses, occupational therapists and other health and social care professionals will be able to gain insight into the new requirements demanded of social workers. Experienced and qualified social workers, and service user and carer-led organisations, especially those contributing to practice learning, will also be able to use this book for consultation, teaching and revision, and to gain insight into the expectations raised by the qualifying degree in social work.

Requirements for social work education

Social work education has undergone a major transformation to ensure that qualified social workers are educated to honours degree level and develop knowledge, skills and values which are common and shared. A vision for social work operating in complex human situations has been adopted. This is reflected in the following definition from the International Association of Schools of Social Work and International Federation of Social Workers (2001):

> The social work profession promotes social change, problem solving in human relationships and the empowerment and liberation of people to enhance well-being. Utilising theories of human behaviour and social systems, social work intervenes at the points where people interact with their environments. Principles of human rights and social justice are fundamental to social work.

This definition encapsulates the notion that social work concerns individual people and wider society, working with people who are vulnerable and may be struggling in some way to participate fully in society. Social workers work at the interface between the marginalised individual, and the social and political environment that may have contributed to their marginalisation.

Social workers need to be highly skilled and knowledgeable to work effectively in this context. The government is keen for social work education and practice to improve. In order to improve the quality of both of these aspects of professional social work, it is crucial that you, as a student social worker, develop a rigorous grounding in and understanding of the theories and models underpinning service user and carer involvement. Such knowledge helps social workers to know what to do, when to do it and how to do it, whilst recognising that social work is a complex activity with no absolute 'rights' or 'wrongs' of practice for each situation.

This book will help students to meet the demands outlined by the Department of Health in the prescribed curriculum, and especially in relation to the expressed need that all social workers must involve service users and carers in social work practice.

The book will help to meet the Quality Assurance Agency subject benchmark statements for social work. These include being able to understand the nature of social work and developing knowledge and understanding about the following:

- social work services and social work users;

- values and ethics;

- social work theory;

- the nature of social work practice.

The book will also help to meet the National Occupational Standards (NOS) set for social workers. The standards state clearly that operational process skills are central to competence. Social workers must:

- prepare for work with people and assess their needs and circumstances;

- plan, carry out, review and evaluate in social work;

- support individuals to represent needs, views and circumstances;

- manage risk;

- be accountable with supervision and support for own practice;

- demonstrate professional competence in social work practice.

In essence, the book will concentrate on models of service user and carer participation that are current in practice and transferable across different settings. These models are active, practical and open to evaluation. Case studies, which focus on a range of young and adult service users and carers, will be used throughout to enhance this process and to illustrate key points.

Book structure

There are six core chapters to this book. We begin in Chapter 1 by taking a broad approach to the participation of service users and carers in social work practice, thereby setting a context for this particular area of practice. You will be asked to reflect on what is meant by the term 'service user and carer participation' and to identify some of the opportunities that exist within social work practice for service users and carers to become involved. In considering who participates, there will be opportunities for you to reflect upon whose voices may not be so readily heard, and to consider some of the factors that may prevent individuals and groups from participating more fully in social work practice. From this you will be asked to consider why participation is important and to explore some of the practical benefits to services.

Chapter 2 focuses on the origins and development of service user and carer involvement and participation, providing an historical and legal context to your learning. In this chapter, you will be able to trace the development of different service users' and carers' movements within the United Kingdom and, where appropriate, make comparisons with international developments. Charting such developments can be particularly helpful in highlighting the ways in which service user and carer movements have been associated with major changes in legislation, social policy, culture, social work theory and service provision. From this you will be asked to examine the legal and policy framework underpinning individual and collective involvement in social work practice.

The question whether or not involvement is real and full rather than tokenistic is a central theme of this book. In Chapter 3 there will be opportunities for you to examine some of the different approaches and models to participation that have been adopted, and to explore the varying degrees or levels of participation and power afforded to service users and carers in practice. You will also be asked to examine some of the barriers or challenges to service user and carer participation, and to reflect on the key characteristics of effective participatory practice. The chapter will conclude by considering what needs to change organisationally for participation to become more meaningful.

Chapter 4 highlights the importance of empowering service users' and carers' participation. The approach and value base of individual practitioners is an important feature of empowering practice. Opportunities will be provided for you to reflect on your own personal feelings and attitudes towards service user and carer participation, particularly with regard to sharing power and helping to increase control over people's lives. Current research about service user and carer perceptions of social workers will be provided to help you to gain insight into some of the desirable qualities and attributes that service users and carers have said that they would like to see in a social worker. Effective participation is also dependent upon strong organisational commitment to the values and principles of involvement. The chapter will, therefore, also examine the values and principles underpinning social work practice, and provide opportunities for you to consider how these values and principles can be put into action to make service user and carer involvement for organisations and services a reality.

Chapter 5 considers some of the ways and means of facilitating adult service user and carer involvement. In this chapter you will examine some of the key components required for building and sustaining effective participation, focusing in particular on organisational infrastructure, the building and sustaining of positive relationships, and the development of effective support mechanisms. There will also be opportunities to explore some of the different methods and approaches that can be used to develop participatory practices with adult service users and carers. This will help you to develop ways of working that promote service user and carer participation.

The specific issues surrounding the involvement of children and young people in social work practice, and some of the mechanisms that can be employed in working with these service user and carer groups, will be explored in Chapter 6. In this chapter, there will be opportunities for you to examine some of the challenges facing the social worker in learning to adopt appropriate support roles and in working in ways that are child-centred. You will also be asked to identify the key skills that are required of practitioners in enabling the participation of children and young people both in collective and individual decision-making processes, and to reflect on aspects of your own skill development.

Concluding remarks and signposts will be offered at the end of the book. At this stage you will be invited to review the learning outcomes set for the chapters. You will be encouraged to chart and monitor your learning, taking developmental needs and reflections forward to other books within the series.

Learning features

This book is interactive. You are encouraged to work through each chapter as an active participant, taking responsibility for your learning in order to increase your knowledge, understanding and ability to apply this learning to your practice with service users and carers. You will be expected to reflect creatively on how your immediate learning needs can be met in the areas of service user participation and involvement, and how your professional learning can be developed to ensure full and genuine participation of service users and carers in your future career.

Case studies throughout the book will help you to examine the concepts, theories and models that underpin service user and carer involvement and participation in social work practice. Activities have been devised that require you to reflect on experiences, situations and events, and help you to review and summarise learning undertaken. In this way your knowledge will become deeply embedded as part of your development. When you come to undertake social work practice with service users and carers, the work and reflection undertaken here will help you to improve and hone your skills and knowledge.

This book will introduce knowledge and learning activities for you as a student social worker concerning some of the central processes relating to issues of daily practice in all areas of the discipline. Suggestions for further reading and research are made at the end of each chapter.

Professional development and reflective practice

Great emphasis is placed on developing skills of reflection about, in and on practice. The idea of reflective practice has developed over many years in social work. It is important also that you reflect prior to and during practice. This book will assist you in developing a questioning approach that looks in a critical way at your thoughts, experiences and practice, and seeks to heighten your skills in refining your practice as a result of these deliberations. Reflection is central to good social work practice, but only if action results from that reflection.

Reflecting about, in and on your practice is not only important during your education to become a social worker, it is considered key to continued professional development. As we move to a profession that acknowledges lifelong learning as a way of keeping up to date, of ensuring that research informs practice and of honing skills and values for practice, it is important to begin the process at the outset of your learning and development. The importance of professional development is clearly shown by its inclusion in the National Occupational Standards and is reflected in the General Social Care Council (GSCC) Code of Practice for Employees.

Chapter 1

Understanding service user and carer involvement and participation

ACHIEVING A SOCIAL WORK DEGREE

This chapter will help you to meet the following National Occupational Standards (see the Skills for Care website, **www.skillsforcare.org.uk**):

Key Role 1: Prepare for, and work with individuals, families, carers, groups and communities to assess their needs and circumstances.

- Work with individuals, families, carers, groups and communities to help them make informed decisions.
- Assess needs and options to recommend a course of action.

Key Role 2: Plan, carry out, review and evaluate social work practice, with individuals, families, carers, groups, communities and other professionals.

- Respond to crisis situations.
- Interact with individuals, families, carers, groups and communities to achieve change and development and to improve life opportunities.
- Prepare, produce, implement and evaluate plans with individuals, families, carers, groups, communities and professional colleagues.
- Support the development of networks to meet assessed needs and planned outcomes.
- Work with groups to promote individual growth, development and independence.

Key Role 3: Support individuals to represent their needs, views and circumstances.

- Advocate with, and on behalf of, individuals, families, carers, groups and communities.
- Prepare for, and participate in decision-making forums.

Key Role 4: Manage risk to individuals, families, carers, groups, communities, self and colleagues.

- Assess and manage risks to individuals, families, carers, groups and communities.

Key Role 5: Manage and be accountable, with supervision and support, for your own social work practice within your organisation.

- Contribute to the management of resources and services.
- Manage, present and share records and reports.

Key Role 6: Demonstrate professional competence in social work practice.

- Research, analyse, evaluate, and use current knowledge of best social work practice.
- Manage complex ethical issues, dilemmas and conflicts.

It will also introduce you to the following academic standards as set out in the social work subject benchmark statements:

3.1.1 Social work services and service users

- The nature of social work services in a diverse society.
- The relationship between agency policies, legal requirements and professional boundaries in shaping the nature of services provided in inter-disciplinary contexts and the issues associated with working across professional boundaries and within different disciplinary groups.

3.1.2 The service delivery context

- The issues and trends in modern public and social policy and their relationship to contemporary practice and service delivery in social work.
- The significance of legislative and legal frameworks and service delivery standards.
- The current range and appropriateness of statutory, voluntary and private agencies providing community-based, day-care, residential and other services and the organisational systems inherent within these.

3.1.3 Values and ethics

- The moral concepts of rights, responsibility, freedom, authority and power inherent in the practice of social workers as moral and statutory agents.

3.1.4 Social work theory

- Research-based concepts and critical explanations from social work theory and other disciplines that contribute to the knowledge base of social work.

3.1.5 The nature of social work practice

- The place of theoretical perspectives and evidence from international research in assessment and decision-making processes in social work practice.

The subject skills highlighted to demonstrate this knowledge in practice include:

3.2.2 Problem-solving skills

3.2.2.1 Managing problem-solving activities.

3.2.2.2 Gathering information.

3.2.2.3 Analysis and synthesis.

3.2.2.4 Intervention and evaluation.

3.2.3 Communication skills

- Listen actively to others, engage appropriately with the life experiences of service users, understand accurately their viewpoint and overcome personal prejudices to respond appropriately to a range of complex personal and interpersonal situations.

3.2.4 Skills in working with others

- Involve users of social work services in ways that increase their resources, capacity and power to influence factors affecting their lives.
- Consult actively with others, including service users, who hold relevant information or expertise.
- Act co-operatively with others, liaising and negotiating across differences such as organisational and professional boundaries and differences of identity or language.
- Develop effective helping relationships and partnerships with other individuals, groups and organisations that facilitate change.

5.2.1 Knowledge and understanding

- Ability to use this knowledge and understanding in work within specific practice contexts.

Introduction

Participation and involvement of service users and carers has become a key issue in current social work policy, practice, research and education. Over the past two decades, there has been a marked increase in the involvement of service users and carers in the provision of health and social care services across the United Kingdom. This involvement has taken place in many different forms, including:

- individual care planning, service delivery and review;

- the planning and development of services;

- the organisation and management of social work and social care;

- the development of service user and carer-led initiatives;

- staff and student training;

- research.

Service user and carer participation in shaping and developing health and social care services throughout England and Wales has been a central theme in the government's modernisation agenda (see, for example, Department of Health, 1998a, 2000b, 2001b). The need for involvement in the planning, development, provision and arrangement of social and health care services originates from a long-standing concern about raising standards in service delivery, so that services can be improved and become more effective in meeting complex and diverse needs. In consequence, service user and carer involvement and influence now extend across the full spectrum of services for children and families, people with disabilities, older people's and mental health service provision.

The involvement of service users and carers in health and social care education is essential to the development of service user and carer participation in practice. Indeed, the importance of service user and carer participation has been recognised in the government's reform of social work education. As you may already be aware from your own training experiences, higher education institutions that offer social work training programmes are now required *to involve service users and carers as stakeholders in all parts of the design and delivery of the programme* (Levin, 2004, p3). This is important so that trainee social workers can *gain a thorough grounding in service users' and carers' experiences and expectations from the very start of their training and careers* (Levin, 2004, p2), and can develop and deliver a better service. The new social work qualifying degree, therefore, focuses on how academic learning can support practice by better equipping social work practitioners to include service users and carers in decision-making processes that affect their own lives. This is important, for if the quality of services is to be improved, all newly qualified social workers need to know how to make services more sensitive to the needs and preferences of the individuals who use them, and how to extend the capacity of service users and carers to participate in decisions about service design, management and review.

Being skilled in working in partnership is a key requirement for social workers. This is reflected in the Teaching, Learning and Assessment Requirements for Social Work Training:

> As well as providing teaching, learning and assessment across the full range of the occupational standards and benchmark statement, providers will have to demonstrate that all students undertake specific learning and assessment in the following key areas:
>
> - *partnership working and information sharing across professional disciplines and agencies.*

(DoH, 2002b, pp3–4)

Partnership working, in this context, does not just refer to working together with professionals from other disciplines and agencies. It refers also to the need for social workers to work alongside service users and carers, engaging them as partners in, for example, jointly planning services or jointly assessing situations and negotiating the delivery of services. The building and sustaining of such partnerships demands increased levels of power sharing and equality, a theme that will be returned to in Chapters 3 and 4 when we explore different models of participatory practice, and the concept of empowering service user and carer participation.

It may be worth considering for a moment some of the specific gains that arise from involving service users and carers in the professional training of social workers.

ACTIVITY 1.1

Why might it be helpful for service users and carers to be involved in training social workers?

List as many reasons as you can for involving service users and carers in training people.

If you are not currently involved in a training programme, think about what you could gain personally from training that is delivered by a service user or carer.

Comment

There is a number of positive reasons or benefits that you could have listed, so don't worry if what you have written does not quite correspond with what follows. The gains identified below have been drawn from a report that was produced in 1994 to provide guidance on the development of policy and practice to increase service user involvement in social work training (Beresford, 1994). The list, however, can be applied equally well to the involvement of service users and carers in social work training today. Generally, the participation and involvement of service users and carers provide us with opportunities to:

- value service users and carers for who they are. It is important that we recognise the contribution that they can make, the benefits that participation can bring to our organisations and the people whom we work with, and the ways in which participation can enable us to undertake our work more effectively.

- learn about the particular expertise, ideas and experience of service users and carers. They have unique knowledge, expertise and experience of disability, service delivery, oppression and discrimination, which cannot be obtained elsewhere. Their insights into practice and how it may be improved, are an important social work training resource.

- see people who use services and their carers in positive active roles as contributors, informers and educators. This may challenge our perceptions of service users and carers as passive and dependent, or people with problems, and offers us alternative models upon which to base our relationships with them.

- exchange ideas and develop working partnerships between service users, service agencies, students and educators.

- align the theories of social work intervention with practice, highlighting underpinning assumptions and values. Jargon and professional stereotypes can be challenged and theories can be evaluated within the context of everyday life.

- ensure that social work training is appropriate, relevant, sensitive and fit for purpose. Such training needs to safeguard people's rights and ensure the development of skills and competencies that service users and carers value.

(Adapted from *Changing the culture: Involving service users in social work education,* Beresford, 1994 with permission from Peter Beresford, Professor of Social Policy, Brunel University and Chair of Shaping Our Lives, the national service user controlled organisation and network.)

In this chapter, you will be introduced to some of the ways in which service user and carer participation is understood. The concept of service user involvement is complex and has been debated and contested over many years. You will be introduced to some of the definitional perspectives and invited to consider some of the opportunities that exist within social work practice for service user and carer participation and involvement. In considering who participates, it is important to develop an awareness of individuals and groups of people whose views may not be so readily heard, and to consider some of the factors that may prevent their full participation or involvement. There will be opportunities to explore the reasons why it is important to include service users and carers in shaping services, and to consider some of the practical benefits of participation both for service users and carers, and service providers. Contemporary guidance and advice on service user and carer participation will be provided, and there will be activities to help you to make links between knowledge and practice throughout the chapter. Case studies, based on anonymised service user and carer statements, will be combined with practice examples to illustrate some of the concepts and processes involved. You will be asked to question the purpose and value of service user and carer involvement and participation, and consider the importance of putting service users and carers at the heart of social work practice. This will provide you with knowledge that you can usefully use when we move on in later chapters to consider different models of participation, and how we can promote genuine service user and carer involvement and participation in social work practice.

What is service user and carer participation? Definitional perspectives

Learning about service user and carer participation, how to involve participants and develop skilled competence in working together with service users and carers is central to your development as a social worker. Before you can begin learning these skills, however, it is important to have some idea of what we mean by service user and carer participation, how service users and carers are defined, and by whom.

This section introduces some of the ways in which service user and carer participation might be understood. It is important to have an awareness of different understandings or perspectives of participation because this can affect who is involved, how participation takes place, how information or knowledge gained from this process is used and what action results from such involvement. Moreover, how you view service user and carer participation will affect the ways in which you work and equally important, how service users and carers perceive that process will impact on how they work with you.

So what do we mean when we talk about service user and carer participation? Braye notes that:

> the language of participation is complex: the same term means different things to different people, and the same concept may be known by a number of different terms.

> (Braye, 2000, p9)

The terms 'participation', 'partnership', 'involvement' and 'working together' are often used to encapsulate a wide range of different ideas and activities. These terms may sometimes be used interchangeably or can have different meanings for different people, there being no universally accepted definition. In this book, you will notice that all of these words are used to describe the inclusion of service users and carers in social work practice. We will return to this discussion about the use of language in Chapter 3 when we consider degrees or varying levels of participation, but for now what is important to remember is this: whatever word or phrase any of us chooses to use, the challenge for all of us is how to put into practice the ideas underpinning these terms. For as Braye states:

> The terminology is less important than the intention behind the actions it describes.

> (Braye, 2000, p9)

Traditionally, social workers have seen their clients in a 'worker–helper' relationship, with the social worker as helper and the client as helped (see Jordon, 1982). In such a paternalist relationship, the practitioner, who was seen as 'the expert', defined both the purpose and manner of involvement (Howe, 1992) and the course of action that was to be taken. Such practice, however, confirmed a view of service users as both dependent (Beresford, 1994) and passive (Howe, 1992). In training, student social workers would intervene in service users' lives during times of difficulty and crisis, when the focus was on problems, failings or inadequacies, rather than service users' abilities, strengths, resources and capacities (Beresford, 1994). Such a relationship confirmed a rather biased view of service users as weak and vulnerable.

The 1980s and 1990s, however, witnessed a shift in the client–worker relationship, with greater emphasis being placed on the rights and abilities of clients to define and understand their own situation. Within such a participatory framework, social workers began to actively involve clients in defining the problem or need, understanding the situation and deciding the plan of action to be taken (see Howe, 1992). The recognition that worker and client possessed 'different knowledges and skills' led to an increased willingness by professionals to see clients as 'active and equal partners' (see Howe, 1992). These changes were part of a broader shift in thinking, and increased involvement of service users and carers in social work, social services and other public services. This took many different forms, including people having a greater say and involvement in their personal dealings with social services, in the management of those services and in the planning of new services (Beresford, 1994).

The origins and development of service user and carer involvement and participation in social work practice will be explored further in Chapter 2. What is important to note here, however, is that these developments impacted on the way in which individual professionals and organisations interacted with service users, and as the relationship between social services staff and service users changed, so too did the language used to define those relationships. For some workers, the term 'client', with its overtones of professionalism, expertise and control (see Corrigan and Leonard, 1978, cited in Heffernan, 2006, p140), failed to define the more equitable kind of relationship that they aimed to develop in their practice. In consequence, the terms 'service user' and 'carer' became part of the vocabulary of social work and social care, this change in the use of language reflecting the principles underpinning 'user involvement' and participation in social work practice – that services should be 'user-centred', 'needs-led' and 'user-led'.

Defining the terms 'service user' and 'carer'

In developing an understanding of the groups and individuals identified by these terms, it is important to acknowledge that we are not talking about a homogenous group of people but different groups of people with different sets of needs. In this sense, the terms 'service users' or 'carers' represent umbrella or shorthand terms (Beresford, 2000). Think for a moment about how you might define the terms 'service user' and 'carer'.

ACTIVITY 1.2

How would you define 'service user' and 'carer'?

Complete the statement 'I believe a service user is...'. Then write out the statement four more times and complete each sentence in a different way.

Similarly, complete five different statements that begin 'I believe a carer is...'.

When you have done this, write a brief summary of each of your list of statements.

Comment

Defining a service user

Historically, the term 'service user' has focused on only those people who currently receive services and support, either voluntarily or involuntarily from the public, voluntary and private sectors, or have done so in the past, in order to carry out ordinary daily activities. This embraces people included in a wide range of categories, such as:

- mental health service users;

- people living with HIV/AIDS;

- children and young people who have experience of being looked after in care;

- people with a physical disability or sensory impairment;

- older people;

- people with learning difficulties;

- people with experience of multiple impairments (for example, people with physical impairments and learning difficulties; people with experience of using both mental health services and of physical impairments);

- people using palliative care services;

- people with a dependency on drugs or alcohol;

- people with experience as refugees.

Broader, more inclusive definitions of the term 'service user' have emerged which include those people who are *eligible* to receive social care and social work services (Beresford, 2000) as well as:

> those who define themselves as potential users of social work services, either because they anticipate a future need, or because they choose not to use the services that are currently available to them.

(Swift, 2002, cited in Levin, 2004, p19)

Beresford (2000, p489) highlights that the term 'service user' is problematic because it views people *primarily in terms of their use of services, which may not be how they would define themselves*. Service user organisations, such as Shaping Our Lives National User Network, give their own definitions:

> The term 'service user' can be used to restrict your identity as if all you are is a passive recipient of health and welfare services. That is to say, a service user can be seen as someone who has things 'done to them' or who quietly accepts and receives a service. This makes it seem that the most important thing about you is that you use or have used services. It ignores all the other things you do and which make up who you are as a person.

(Shaping Our Lives National User Network, 2003)

They advocate that a service user should always be self-identifying and seen as a person first and foremost, but recognise that it is the shared experience of using services that provides a strong voice to improve service provision and delivery.

Defining a 'carer'

The term 'carer' distinguishes those people who provide care for others on an unpaid basis, from those who are paid (care workers, home helps, people employed by someone with a disability). Whilst traditionally, this group of people has been referred to as 'informal' or 'family' carers, carers tell us that they do not like the word 'informal' (see Nolan, Grant and Keady, 1996), and experience suggests that not all carers are family members. Carers' organisations, therefore, favour more inclusive definitions:

> Carers look after family, partners or friends in need of help because they are ill, frail or have a disability. The care they provide is unpaid.

(Carers UK, 2005)

> A carer is someone, who, without payment, provides help and support to a partner, child, relative, friend or neighbour, who could not manage without their help. This could be due to age, physical or mental illness, addiction or disability.

(The Princess Royal Trust for Carers, 2005)

A carer may, therefore, be a relative, partner, child, friend or neighbour who provides, or intends to provide, practical care or emotional support to someone who is unable to care for themselves. The person with care needs may be frail, have a learning or physical disability, a long-term or terminal illness, a mental illness, or be dependent on drugs or alcohol. Like service users, *carers come from all walks of life, all cultures and can be any age* (The Princess Royal Trust for Carers, 2005).

Children and young people under the age of 18 who provide, or intend to provide care, assistance or support to another family member have become known as 'young carers'. Whilst not every child whose parent, sibling or relative is ill or disabled is necessarily a young carer, some children and young people:

> carry out, often on a regular basis, significant or substantial caring tasks and assume a level of responsibility which would usually be associated with an adult. The person receiving care is often a parent but can be a sibling, grandparent or other relative who is disabled, has some chronic illness, mental health problem or other condition connected with a need for care, support or supervision.

(Becker, 2000, p378)

Many young and adult carers do not, in fact, think of themselves as carers – they are just giving help to their mother, son or partner, just 'caring' and *doing what anyone else would in the same position* (The Princess Royal Trust for Carers, 2005). Research and practice have shown that some carers choose to take on the task voluntarily, others are informally nominated, usually by family members and, in some families, it is demanded. The majority, however, just grow into the role as highlighted in the young carers' research literature.

RESEARCH SUMMARY

Children socialised into caring roles

Research undertaken by the Young Carers Research Group at Loughborough University found that young carers who had been socialised from an early age into their caring roles, defined their various duties (many of them of an intimate nature) as everyday routines (Aldridge and Becker, 1993). In such circumstances, some children and young people may see themselves as young carers but others do not.

Therefore, as Frank (2002) suggests, it is important for professionals to recognise that there are different perspectives on the definition of a young carer and to listen to the young people's points of view about definition and perception. She notes that when asked, children tend to describe their situations in terms of feelings and tasks rather than attempt a definition of 'young carer'.

In the following case study, we see how Susan, a young carer, has been socialised into her caring role from an early age. She has no specific memories about the onset of parental illness, her awareness and understanding being developed gradually over time.

Susan, aged 14, has cared for her mum, who has schizophrenia, for as long as she can remember. Her first recollection of her mum's illness was:

Probably from around four [years old]. Well, I remember she just used to do unusual things sometimes and I remember having to look after her a few times ... when she weren't well. I just stayed with her and made sure she didn't do anything ... stupid or nothing.

Throughout much of her life, Susan has generally kept an eye on her mum and helped with domestic tasks around the home, including the shopping. These responsibilities have resulted in Susan missing school for substantial amounts of time.

More recently, Susan has met with other young people in similar caring roles at a specialist young carers' group. Before this experience, she never really thought about what she did to help at home and did not identify herself as a carer – her caring role was just a normal part of her everyday life.

Diversity of the service user and carer voice

In developing service user and carer involvement in social care services, it is important for us to remember that we are working with a range of views and experiences. There is no 'one' service user or carer voice, and neither the service user nor carer movements are united or unified bodies. As Molyneux and Irvine note:

Good practice guidelines drawn up by the Association of Directors of Social Services (Jones, 1995) suggest that it should be recognised that users and carers contribute views and perspectives based on their own experiences. They may be representative, or typical users, but not necessarily be able to be the representative of others. The legitimacy of their views rests in their personal experience, and it is likely that those in similar circumstances will share much of that experience.

(Molyneux and Irvine, 2004, p295)

What opportunities are there for participation in social work practice?

Service user and carer participation in social work practice requires established and regular opportunities for involvement, as well as informal or occasional opportunities (Youll and McCourt-Perrin, 1993). It is possible for service users and carers to be involved at any stage in assessment, research, decision-making, planning, review or development. They can participate at an individual level through, for example, assessment and planning processes, or they can contribute collectively as in strategic planning processes or the provision of user-led services. The key to involvement and participation, therefore, is to create a range of opportunities, so that service users and carers have a choice about how and when they become involved, and can contribute whatever they feel able to.

It is worth thinking for a moment about the potential opportunities that exist for service user and carer involvement and participation:

ACTIVITY **1.3**

How might service users and carers participate in social work practice?

Think about the range of arenas in social work and social care in which service users and carers could potentially participate. You might like to record your list in the form of a mind-map. For example,

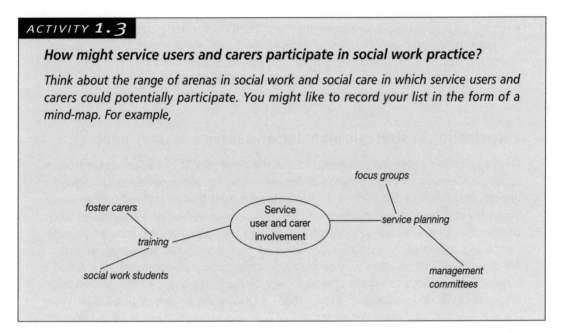

Comment

In constructing your mind-map, we hope that you will have thought about participation by service users and carers in their own use of services, in strategic planning and development, research or service evaluation, training of staff and student social workers, and participation through the development of user led services. We will now consider each of these opportunities in turn.

Participation in own use of services

At an individual 'consumer' level, community care legislation has given adult service users the right to involvement in constructing their own care or support packages. The legislation underpinning service provision for children and young people also says that their views should be taken into account, whilst the legal and policy framework concerning carers places emphasis on involving and consulting them with regard to the services that they need. All of the decision-making processes about the provision of care and support to an individual – assessment, care planning and review – provide opportunities for children, young people and adults to have a say in their own services, and to exercise choice and control over their use of those services.

- *Assessment* – involving individual service users or carers in their assessment of need ensures that their wishes and feelings are heard from the outset.

- *Planning and purchasing of services* – this may, to varying degrees, involve the individuals concerned. In some situations, more extensive levels of participation are evident.

Direct payments, for example, enable people with disabilities, people with learning difficulties, mental health service users and older people to use local authority funds to purchase their own assistance independently of the local authority.

- *Review of care plans* – provides regular opportunities for participation to determine whether a care plan and the services received meet, and will continue to meet, an individual's needs, and whether changes may be necessary. Research highlights the importance of creatively engaging service users in continual consultation and review of their care and support (Carr, 2004).

Participation in strategic planning and service development

Service users and carers can also contribute to the development of services at the level of strategic planning through a range of forums including planning meetings, advisory groups, management committees, strategic development groups and stakeholder meetings. Each of these forms of involvement provides opportunities for service users and carers to offer their perspective of services, either based on their own personal knowledge, experience and expertise, or as a representative of a service user organisation or group. Alternatively, service planners may develop a planning consultative network, canvassing a range of organisations or groups of service users, to elicit their views, which are then taken into account in future planning (Braye, 2000). Consultation on service plans, Best Value Reviews, service satisfaction surveys or service user and carer involvement in group workshops help to produce more knowledge and understanding, which in turn enable service providers to gain new insights so that they can improve, change and develop services.

As Sartori (2003) states:

> *Where participants have been willing to openly state their concerns about past problems and have discussed solutions used elsewhere, there has been good progress. Health and social care staff have found things out from each other and from service users for the first time and discovered that, despite gulfs in background and experience, everyone has something useful to contribute and that positive outcomes are achievable.*

> (Source: *Community Care*, 13-19 November 2003. Published by permission of the editor of *Community Care*.)

There are many examples nationally of good social work practice in involving adults, young people and children as users of social work services, and also the carers of social work service users in the planning and development of services. Many local authorities have identified a number of methods that actively promote and enable service user and carer participation. These include:

- encouraging a regular service users' or carers' forum;

- inviting service users to sit on forums or working parties that are looking to improve or develop particular parts of a service;

- establishing focus groups of service users and carers;

- involving service users and carers on management committees;

- initiating service users' and carers' conferences.

Gloucestershire County Council promotes ongoing service user and carer involvement in planning and service development through a range of participative methods as the following case study shows.

CASE STUDY

Gloucestershire County Council involves a range of service users and carers in planning and service development:

Carers Gloucestershire
This is a well established, contracted service providing a forum for consultation with, and participation by more than 3,000 carers on issues that affect them. There are also several smaller forums of carers that are affiliated to, or managed by, Carers Gloucestershire.

Carers Consultative Group
Within Carers Gloucestershire, there is a smaller consultative group of 60–70 active members and carer representatives who participate in a range of management and planning forums including:

- *The Mental Health Board;*

- *The Learning Disability Partnership Board;*

- *National Services Framework Board;*

- *Various Health Forums.*

Parent Carers Group
This is an expanding group of parent carers of children and young people with disabilities.

Young Carers Forum
Comments from this group of children and young people are fed into Education and Children's Services and contribute to Children and Young People's Service Planning.

Black Carers Forum
This group, managed by Carers Gloucestershire, has evolved separately. Much work has been undertaken to bring together within the Black Carers Forum, carers from the many different black and minority ethnic communities locally. Whilst this group continues to meet separately to feedback specifically on black and minority ethnic issues, they are also included in an increasing number of mainstream consultations.

Gloucestershire Service User Forum
This project is contracted out by Gloucestershire County Council, enabling it to maintain a degree of independence from the Council's mainstream mechanisms. The forum has contact with over 300 service users and a number of voluntary groups who are themselves in touch with service users. The purpose of the forum is to look at how people are asked about the services that they receive, and to ensure that service users are involved in the training, recruitment and selection of social care staff.

The Service User Forum Steering Group comprises service users from a range of adult services including services for older people; people with mental health issues; people with a sensory

---

---

impairment or physical disability, and people with learning difficulties. Current work is focusing on the best ways of involving children and young people who use social care services, particularly children and young people who are looked after, and those with disabilities.

Opportunities to participate in social care forums within Gloucestershire County Council

There is a number of forums within the organisation for service user and carer involvement.

Locality Group Meetings

There are six locality groups for people with learning disabilities to meet to raise issues of concern and look at how these can be addressed. A report on any issues raised from these meetings is fed through to the Learning Disability Partnership Board.

'Speak Out' Group

This is a mental health services user group, affiliated to the service user forum, that consults regularly with the network of service users.

Young People Looked After Network (YPLAN)

This is a consultation group of looked-after children and young people who meet to look at ways in which they can have a say in decisions that affect them. This group feeds into the Listening to Children Reference Group comprising senior staff, the Lead Member for Children, together with children and young people representatives.

All of these activities feed into the Children and Young People Services Plan.

Conferences

- *Inter-agency County Conference*
  This is a quarterly information-sharing, consultative forum for people with learning disabilities, comprising service users with learning disabilities and staff from all organisations, including social services, health, private and voluntary sector organisations.

- *SUCCESS Conference (Service User Client and Carer Empowerment in Social Services)*
  This is an annual event for all service user and carer groups, staff and councillors to review progress, and to develop plans for service user and carer involvement for the following year.

Participation through the development of user-led services

Since the 1960s there has been a steady growth of independent service provider organisations led and controlled by users at national, regional and local levels. At the national level, examples include the Spinal Injuries Association (SIA), the National Centre for Independent Living and Shaping Our Lives. At a regional level, examples range from groups such as the Essex Coalition of Disabled People, the Wiltshire and Swindon Users' Network, to the Council of Disabled People Warwickshire (CDP). User-controlled organisations, which are independent of the local authority, have often developed in response to users' dissatisfaction with traditional statutory welfare services (Beresford, 1994; Morris, 1994). Such organisations provide a range of community care services, alongside other independent agencies, to support the promotion of independent living. Research suggests that service user-led organisations are far more responsive to people's needs both in terms of what is on offer and how it is delivered, with peer support being a key consideration (Barnes, Morgan and Mercer, 2001). These organisations are also strong and active in pushing for change, applying pressure to many local statutory organisations and businesses to do this, as the following case study highlights.

CASE STUDY

Wiltshire and Swindon Users' Network

The Wiltshire and Swindon Users' Network was set up by long-term service users in 1991 as an independent user-controlled organisation to support users to empower themselves and influence change. It has become an example of good practice nationally and places emphasis on demonstrating innovative examples of user-controlled involvement in social care.

Its Mission Statement is:

> *To promote user involvement and to disseminate examples of good practice in user involvement in Community Care purchasing, provision and evaluation.*

This is done by:

- *supporting the empowerment of users;*

- *enabling users to acts as agents of change;*

- *being proactive in facilitating learning amongst Community Care professionals, voluntary, statutory, and private bodies both county-wide and nationally;*

- *developing and managing user controlled projects.*

Further information can be obtained direct from Wiltshire and Swindon Users' Network, 7 Prince Maurice Court, Hambleton Avenue, Devizes, Wiltshire, SN10 2RT or from their website at www.wsun.co.uk

---

Participation in research or service evaluation

Community care legislation provided opportunities for service users and carers to be involved, at both an individual and a collective level, in the delivery and evaluation of services. As Evans and Fisher (1999, p101) assert:

> *Users' views of the quality of services and their participation in providing regular feedback on all aspects of social work are therefore an essential part of good practice.*

Traditionally, service users' and carers' perspectives on services have been sought by professional researchers and evaluators. In recent years, however, there has been a redistribution of power between those conducting research and those being 'researched'. This has resulted in the involvement of service users in participatory approaches (where users participate in research projects) and emancipatory approaches (where users drive research projects) to research. As Evans and Fisher (1999, p101) state:

As users have become more empowered and experienced in participation, there is a growing understanding of how they can themselves design and undertake such evaluation exercises.

These participatory and emancipatory approaches have led to service users and carers becoming involved in each stage of the research process, including:

- identifying and prioritising research topics through, for example, peer reviewing research proposals;

- commissioning research and influencing research funding through, for example, peer reviewing grant applications;

- developing and designing research projects;

- managing research projects and programmes through, for example, membership of research project steering and advisory groups;

- undertaking research itself;

- interpreting research findings;

- disseminating the results of research;

- providing training and support for service user and carer researchers.

The Sainsbury Centre for Mental Health, Service User Research Enterprises at the Institute of Psychiatry, the Service User Research Group for England (SURGE), the Centre for Disability Studies at Leeds University and INVOLVE are all promoting the active participation of service users in collaborative projects between service users and academics which aim to involve service users in all aspects of research. The Mental Health Foundation has also played a major role in supporting and promoting service user-led research in the mental health sector across the United Kingdom through its *Strategies for Living Initiative* (Faulkner and Layzell, 2000; Nicholls, Wright, Waters and Wells, 2003).

CASE STUDY

An example of service user and carer involvement in research
INVOLVE (formerly Consumers in NHS Research) is an advisory group to the Department of Health. Their role is to promote public involvement in NHS, public health and social care research. They believe that involving members of the public leads to research that is more relevant to people's needs, more reliable and more likely to be used.

Public involvement in research refers to active involvement where people involved are not the 'subjects' of research but are active participants, e.g. on a research steering committee. Active involvement is where research is carried out 'with' or 'by ' members of the public rather than 'to', 'about' or 'for' them.

INVOLVE has about 20 members including users of health and social services, unpaid carers, health and social care managers and academics.

CASE STUDY continued

INVOLVE aims to ensure that public involvement improves the way that:

- *decisions are made about what should be a priority for research;*
- *research is commissioned (chosen and funded);*
- *research is carried out;*
- *research findings are communicated.*

Its objectives include:

- *to develop key alliances and partnerships which can promote greater public involvement in research;*
- *to support members of the public to play an active role in research;*
- *to monitor and assess the effects of public involvement in NHS, public health and social care research.*

Further information can be obtained from www.invo.org.uk

Participation in training staff and student social workers

Service users and carers also participate, as consultants and trainers, in the training of staff working in social care services and in the professional training of students on social work degree programmes. Children and young people who are users of Gloucestershire County Council social care services, for example, act as co-leaders with staff from the training section in delivering *Total Respect* training courses which are mandatory for all social work and social care staff, as well as foster carers. Anglia Ruskin University, a provider of both qualifying and post-qualifying social work training, involves a number of partner agencies in arranging and supporting service user and carer involvement in its portfolio of programmes. Services users and carers attend the management group, advisory and sub-working groups that are responsible for developing assessment, curriculum, recruitment and selection, and quality assurance, as the following case study shows.

CASE STUDY

The systematic involvement of service users and carers in social work training on the BA and MA in Social Work at Anglia Ruskin University
Project aims
The programme aims to systematically involve social care and health care service users and carers in the admission of social work students, in the delivery of their training, assessment of their knowledge and practice, and in the review, evaluation and further development of the social work programme.

CASE STUDY

Project structure

- **Project co-ordinator** – *former or current service user or carer who has responsibility to organise the service user and carer involvement in the programme; to network and to make the project known locally.*

- **Project advisory group (PAG)** – *a group of service users, carers, agency representatives and university staff, led and organised by the service user/carer co-ordinator, that discusses practical ways of involving a variety of service users and carers on the social work programme.*

- **Programme management committee** – *a forum (comprising university staff, service users, carers and employer representatives) for monitoring the overall quality of the student experience across all pathways in the department.*

Aspects of service user and carer involvement within the degree programmes include:

- **Student admissions** – *service users and carers contribute to the admissions process by suggesting questions to be used in the selection of candidates.*

- **Mainstream lecturing** – *service users and carers are involved in the direct training of students through a range of teaching and learning settings: module lectures, seminars, workshops, conferences and inquiry based learning (IBL), where service users and carers are invited to work together with students on simulated practical situations.*

- **Student assessment** – *the project aims to encourage the meaningful involvement of service users and carers in the assessment of students on practice placement. Service users and carers have also contributed to the assessment of modular assignments by developing feedback criteria, and observing and giving feedback to students on group presentations.*

- **Module revision** – *the project aims to encourage the meaningful involvement of service users and carers in the regular evaluation and revision of modules.*

A recent two-year evaluation of the impact of service user and carer involvement in the training of social work students suggests that such involvement is essential to student learning (Ramon and Anghel, 2005). The value of such participation can be seen in the following personal statement, received following a workshop on homelessness and street life at Anglia Ruskin University, led by a user of the services of a local night shelter:

> *I thought Simon was AMAZING! He said some of the most profound things I have ever heard – and as you probably noticed, I was speechless!!! I really thought that was a hugely valuable session and was a breath of fresh air to hear someone talking so honestly and without censoring his thoughts (religion ... women ... valuables ... oh, he is brilliant!).*

> (MA social work student, Anglia Ruskin University)

ACTIVITY **1.4**

Reflect on your own past and current experiences of training.

Can you identify a training session or event when a service user or carer has challenged your ideas and assumptions, or made you think differently about a topic?

Write down what it was that made an impression on you, and how this experience has impacted on you. For example, did it change your ideas about choice, autonomy or decision-making. What do you now do differently as a result of this experience?

If you have no experience of having been trained by a service user or carer, write down some of the reasons why you think this may be so.

Who are the participants?

Inequalities exist both among individuals and within the structure of our society, which prevent some people from participating fully in the life of our society. These individuals do not share full citizenship with regard to the social, economic and political life of the community; they live on the 'margins' of society, with less choice or control over their lives than other members (Webb and Tossell, 1991), and with a corresponding lack of power and influence to redress this imbalance.

Braye (2000) suggests that the patterns of service user and carer participation evident in social work and social care practice are similarly influenced by the structural inequalities and mechanisms of oppression that exist within our society:

Participation in social care provision will reflect the patterns of dominance, inequality and exclusion that are inherent in the structures of wider society. Users of social care provision have needs which arise from and in turn reinforce their exclusion from the sources of power in mainstream society.

(Braye, 2000, pp12–13)

Who is included in decision-making processes about social work practice and who is not, are important in terms of whose views are heard and whose views are not heard. The findings from a recent series of literature reviews about user involvement in promoting change and enhancing the quality of services for older people, children and young people, people with learning difficulties, mental health issues and disabled people show that service users who are marginalised from mainstream services are also found to be under- or unrepresented in participation initiatives that are intended to develop those services (Carr, 2004). So, which individuals and groups of people are being prevented from participating?

ACTIVITY **1.5**

Take a blank sheet of paper and draw a line down the middle so that you have two columns.

Potentially marginalised groups	Factors preventing their participation

Start with the left-hand column. Based upon your current experience and practice, and your knowledge and understanding of the sources of inequality and differing mechanisms of oppression that are present in British society, compile a list of groups of people who are most likely to be marginalised from mainstream services and participation processes.

Then in the right-hand column, make a list of the factors that prevent these people from participating.

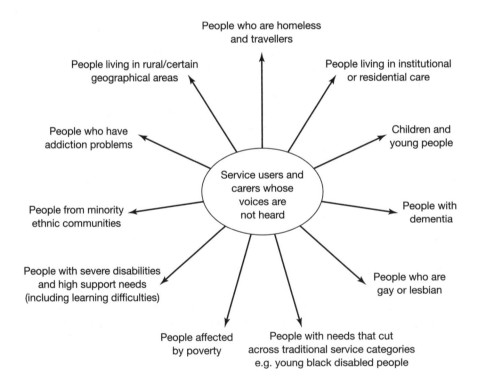

Figure 1.1 Groups who are under-represented in participation processes

Comment

Both structural and cultural barriers contribute to an under-representation of a range of groups of people within both mainstream services and participation processes. These groups include those listed in Figure 1.1.

The barriers to service user and carer participation will be explored in detail in Chapter 3. However, it is important to note here that whilst existing research fails to provide any overview of the barriers to participation by those on the margins of society, pockets of research exist which shed light on some of the obstacles that prevent these service users and carers from shaping services, either individually or collectively:

RESEARCH AND PRACTICE EXAMPLES

Practitioners, managers, policy-makers and planners need to use knowledge critically from research and practice to gain an understanding of the obstacles that might prevent service users and carers from having a voice in evaluating and shaping services. Some of the barriers that have been identified to date include the following.

- *People, such as those in poverty, not being aware that they have a right to a say (ATD Fourth World, 2000, cited in Carr, 2004, p22) about decisions that affect their own lives.*

- *People, such as those with a terminal condition, not wishing to associate themselves publicly with their illness, and/or join national or local groups or associations, and so becoming 'socially invisible' to policy-makers and planners (Small and Rhodes, 2001).*

- *People, such as those who live in poverty or experience multiple oppression, lacking the support, education, self-confidence, self-esteem or the respect of others to make contributions to service planning and development (Evans and Banton, 2001; ATD Fourth World, 2000, cited in Carr, 2004, p22).*

- *People being denied the opportunity to exercise their right to have a say because of:*

  - *a lack of dedicated funding and resources, for example, for black disabled people (British Deaf Association, 1996; Evans and Banton, 2001; Rose, Fleischman, Tonkiss, Campbell and Wykes, 2003);*

  - *a lack of appropriate venues (Danso, Greaves, Howell, Ryan, Sinclair and Tunnard, 2003) or accessible facilities in community meeting places, particularly for people with different impairments (Evans and Banton, 2001);*

  - *a lack of accessible information to inform decision-making, for example, in different minority ethnic languages (Help the Aged, 2001, cited in Janzon and Law, 2003, p14; Danso et al., 2003;) or in British Sign Language video versions for deaf people (British Deaf Association, 1996).*

- *People being stereotyped by service providers (Crawford et al., 2003): for example, white service providers using stereotypes about black families as an excuse not to provide services for black disabled people (Evans and Banton, 2001) or elders from minority ethnic communities (Cordingley, Hughes and Challis, 2001).*

- *Children and young people feeling that formal consultative processes, such as reviews, are run in non-child-friendly ways with adults talking over their heads, making it difficult to express their views (Danso et al., 2003).*

The challenge for mainstream services, therefore, is to engage groups of marginalised people who, as Carr (2004, p22) notes, *seldom have the opportunity to be heard or to influence service change*, and whom agencies find hard to engage. Valuable insights can be gained from the experiences of these marginalised groups of people and yet relatively little is known generally about why people choose to be involved, or why they are excluded. People who are prevented from participating are often labelled 'hard to reach' but as Danso *et al*. (2003) point out, there is a danger in seeing this as something to do with the individuals themselves rather than a reflection of an agency's ability to communicate with a wide range of service users and carers.

Reviewers have identified the considerable research gap that exists regarding knowledge about the exclusion of some groups of people from participation processes. At the time of writing, the Social Care Institute for Excellence's (SCIE) future work on participation includes a project to identify what is meant by the participation of service users who are seldom heard and whom agencies find difficult to engage. This work will focus on identifying the barriers to participation, and assessing the advantages and disadvantages of different models of participation to facilitate the involvement of such service users. More information about this project and SCIE's future work is available from www.scie.org.uk the Institute's website.

Why is service user and carer participation important?

The development of service user and carer participation in health and social care services has been a central theme in the government's reform agenda, the overriding aim of which is to improve the quality of the services that people receive.

Braye (2000) identifies three driving forces behind the development of participatory approaches in social care: the legal and policy mandate; the professional mandate; and the user mandate. She argues that these mandates have arisen from a number of different directions, and consequently, reflect differing ideologies and motivations.

ACTIVITY 1.6

Write down as many reasons as you can think of for social workers, policy-makers, planners, researchers and trainers in social services to involve service users and carers in shaping social work practice. Place these in three lists:

- *reasons that relate to legislation and policy;*

- *reasons that relate to professional practice;*

- *reasons that relate to service user and carer perspectives.*

The legal and policy mandate

The principle of participation underpins much current legislation and policy guidance across the health and social care field. Over the past two decades, several major pieces of legislation have made service user involvement in UK health and social services a statutory duty. The Children Act 1989, the National Health Service and Community Care Act 1990 and the Community Care (Direct Payments) Act 1996 were among some of the first pieces of legislation to make it a statutory requirement to consult and involve those who receive services. These legal mandates were followed by increased requirements for active service user and carer participation in service development and regulation, which were set out in government directives on Best Value for local authorities (Local Government Act 1999), and in the legislation associated with the government's modernisation agenda (Carr, 2004). Participation by service users and carers can be seen in, for example:

- the Quality Protects programme (DoH,1998a);

- Better Care, Higher Standards (DoH, 1999e);

- A Quality Strategy for Social Care (DoH, 2000b);

- Valuing people: A New Strategy for Learning Disability for the Twenty-first Century (DoH, 2001a);

- the National Services Framework for Mental Health (DoH, 1999d), Older People (DoH, 2001b), and, Children, Young People and Maternity Services (DoH, 2004);

- Every Child Matters (DfES, 2003).

The legal and policy mandate through which the principles of service user and carer involvement have been integrated into legal and policy guidance will be explored further in Chapter 2.

Professional mandates

Braye (2000) identifies two distinct strands to the professional mandates that arise from within the social work and social care profession: the first is driven by principle, the second relates to effectiveness.

First, the Code of Practice for Social Care Workers (General Social Care Council, 2002) places a mandate on staff to treat each person as an individual, to support people's rights to control their own lives and to make informed choices about the services that they receive. It also demands that staff promote the independence of service users by, for example, helping them to make complaints. This approach is underpinned by traditional social work values, based on the principles of acceptance; 'respect for persons'; self-deter-mination; individualisation; autonomy and social justice, which demand that people should not be seen as passive recipients of services but treated as active participants in decisions that affect their lives. Alongside these is a professional mandate to promote equal opportunities for service users and carers, respecting diversity, different cultures and values. The social work professional value base acknowledges the structural inequalities that exist in society and the impact that these inequalities have on individuals' life chances. Thus there is a need to tackle such material and structural barriers through approaches that equalise the relationship between users, carers and the providers of a service, and enhance participation. As Braye (2000, p16) suggests:

At the heart of the professional mandate is a will to understand oppression and a commitment to counter it through practice which is participative and empowering.

Braye (2000), however, notes that this professional mandate is constructed upon an assumption of professional power and status, which is evident in the processes of professionally led initiatives to increase service user participation. If involvement by service users and carers is to be successful, then the imbalance in power that exists between users, carers and providers has to be reduced. This is an issue that we will return to in Chapter 3.

Second, whilst there is a general lack of research into and evaluation of the impact and outcomes of service user participation (Carr, 2004), some studies have shown that involving service users and incorporating their views not only has a positive influence on service users' views and experiences of services (Carpenter and Sbaraini, 1997), but also helps to promote more efficient and effective practice (Marsh and Fisher, 1992). This underlines the need for service user and carer participation to be at the heart of professional practice, to ensure that the goals or outcomes of intervention, planning or programme implementation can be achieved.

Service user mandates

Research findings, publications and practice experience suggest that over the past three decades, service users and other marginalised groups have felt excluded from involvement in decision-making processes that affect their lives. There has been a tendency for professionals to place more emphasis on their own professional judgement than on service users' views (Ellis, 1993 and both Hoyes, Means, Lart and Taylor, 1994, cited in Nocon and Qureshi, 1998, p51). As a consequence, there have been demands from those using services for greater involvement in the decisions that affect the nature of the support that they receive, both with regard to self-definition of need (Morris, 1993) and in determining how those needs are to be met (Morris, 1998). Emphasis has been placed on individuals being more able to make choices and to exercise control over their lives (Lindow and Morris, 1995). At a broader level, some service users and user-led organisations have also expressed a wish for greater participation in service planning, so that they can help to design services that more appropriately meet service users' needs (Croft and Beresford, 1990, cited in Nocon and Qureshi, 1998, p52).

New philosophies such as normalisation, the social model of disability, and survivors' perspectives on mental health, which underpin demands for greater levels of involvement and participation in decision-making, challenge the dominant paradigms upon which provision has been traditionally based. These alternative models seek to understand service users' experiences by reference to the social, cultural and physical structures within society that create barriers, and restrict people's options and activities (Carr, 2004). As a result, the service user movement emphasises people's social, political and civil rights as citizens to the benefits and services of the welfare state, and their participation in planning and decision-making processes as fundamental to active citizenship.

What are the benefits of service user and carer participation?

There is intrinsic value for people to be involved in decisions that affect their lives. Improving services via partnership with service users and carers also promotes the development of professional practice and benefits organisations. On the basis of what you have read and considered so far in this chapter, think about the advantages of participation for service users, carers and service providers.

---

*ACTIVITY **1.7***

Draw a table with three headings:

What are the benefits of service user and carer involvement?

Benefits for service users	Benefits for carers	Benefits for service providers

---

Comment

In considering the potential benefits, you may have included the following.

Potential benefits to service users and carers

With regard to the range of potential benefits of participation to service users and carers, you may have included that it:

- *influences the provision of services* – involvement provides an opportunity for people to have a say in matters that directly affect their lives;

- *increases confidence and raises self-esteem* – the practice of self-advocacy, speaking up and voicing one's own opinion can help to build confidence and self-belief (Danso et al., 2003; Janzon and Law, 2003);

- *develops self-help and mutual support* – service users and carers may be more sensitive to, and tolerant of, other users or carers with similar experiences – they may empathise with particular forms of exclusion experienced by those who are disenfranchised (Young, Ackerman and Kyle, 1998);

- *provides a personal 'therapeutic' experience* – involvement enables people to feel that they are being listened to and that their contribution is valued (Welsh Assembly Government, 2004);

- *empowers through collective involvement* – working collectively as part of a network can empower people to instigate change and improvement in their own provision of services (Carr, 2004);

- *provides opportunities for learning* – participation can increase knowledge and enhance skills, education and employment opportunities (Danso et al., 2003);

- *provides new role models* – the presence of deaf adults, for example, in services for deaf children helps to increase children's confidence through recognising themselves in some of the adults around them (Young, Ackerman and Kyle, 1998);

- *promotes advocacy* – involvement enables people to support and assist others in the community to access health and social care services;

- *develops peer-led initiatives* – participation encourages the development of new initiatives that are 'user-centred' and promote the rights and needs of service users and carers.

Potential benefits to service providers

In considering the potential benefits to service providers, you may have identified that involvement of service users and carers can lead to:

- *recognition of service users and carers as experts by their experience* – no one else can have the same experience, the same initial contact with services or the same journey (Welsh Assembly Government, 2004) through the social work or social care system;

- *traditional assumptions being challenged* – service users and carers hold a unique body of knowledge, which can be used to educate staff, thereby dispelling stereotypes (Young, Ackerman and Kyle, 1998);

- *more effective two-way communication* – involvement promotes more effective communication between service users, carers and service providers; information or feedback, for example, can be disseminated quickly and more easily through peer networks;

- *more effective partnerships* – involvement can enhance understanding and improve relationships between service users, carers and staff (Marsh and Fisher, 1992);

- *better targeted services* – service users and carers bring their own unique perspectives of services and support, which can be used to develop better ways of meeting need.

One problem that has been highlighted in the literature is the propensity for agencies to focus on the 'intrinsic benefits' of participation – that is, how service users and carers have gained personally from the experience of participation, rather than on the changes achieved (Carr, 2004). Intrinsic benefits are important, as is knowledge of an individual's experience of the participation process, for as Carr (2004) notes, agencies can learn from both positive and negative responses to improve the process. However, as Danso et al. conclude (2003, p13), we need to ensure that:

> *participation is not simply an end in itself but a means to change.*

It is important, therefore, for agencies to respond to what service users and carers have said during the participation process – as outcomes, impacts on improvement and change, as a result of participation, are the primary purposes of participation.

Before we turn in the next chapter to a discussion of the origins and development of service user and carer involvement and participation in social work practice, consider the following activity.

ACTIVITY *1.8*

Read the two case studies below and think about:

- *the different life experiences of William, a former carer, and Gita, a current service user;*

and

- *the knowledge and skills that they have acquired through these experiences.*

Draw a table with four headings and enter your ideas as they occur to you:

	William	Gita
Knowledge		
Skills		

Case Study 1: William Betteridge

William is 74 years old, white and a widower. He took early retirement over 16 years ago when his wife, Sarah, was first diagnosed with Alzheimer's. He provided full-time care for Sarah at home for over seven years. Sarah was subsequently admitted to long-term care. She died last year. William writes:

It had been found, in some instances in the early 1990s, that carers' views were often ignored and carers had become casualties themselves, especially among the elder population. My comments (about social workers) is that in general, they tried to do their best but many of them did seem to lack some knowledge of carers' issues and the impact that the Carers Act would have ... Most carers were unaware that they had rights too of being heard and were not advised about it at an early stage ... Social workers had already established their own practices of what action to take with the user and seemed unaware of the carers' views and, in a few instances, if they were given, seemed to ignore them. In a nutshell, they were good at dealing with the user but not the carer. When carers' themselves became aware of their rights under the Carers Act, then things began to change for carers. Social workers were well aware of the user, what he or she was entitled to, and what help should be given once the assessment had been made. However, they needed guidance on what help and advice they should give carers and to take carers' views into consideration. In some instances changes had to be made. Once the carers' views were accepted, it created a better view of the situation for all parties.

Case Study 2: Gita East

Gita is 14 and of dual heritage. She is an intelligent, articulate girl who enjoys her studies at a local secondary school. Two years ago, there were reasonable grounds to suggest that she was beyond her mother's control, and she was subsequently made the subject of a full care order. She has since lived in several foster homes and a residential care home. She writes:

They (the social workers) kept saying this is your review, it's your chance to have your say but its just a load of rubbish. They're supposed to listen but they don't. They've already made up their minds, they don't like to listen to what you've got to say at all. They're just like doing this (the review) because they've got to.

Then, with reference to William and Gita's knowledge, skills and experience, and your own knowledge gained through this chapter, compile a list of the ways in which William and Gita could become involved in participation processes.

27

Comment

This activity will help you to consolidate your knowledge. We have not provided examples of what you may have found here as this gives you an opportunity to check through your understanding of this chapter. You do need, however, to bear in mind the following questions:

- What further information might you need or wish to explore?

- How might you obtain this information?

C   H   A   P   T   E   R   S   U   M   M   A   R   Y

In this chapter you have been introduced to some of the complexities in service user and carer involvement and participation through a series of key questions. First, we considered the question, 'What is service user and carer participation?', and in thinking about some definitional perspectives, we acknowledged the diversity of the service user and carer voice. Second, we asked, 'What opportunities are there for participation in social work practice?' This question helped you to identify a range of arenas in social work and social care in which service users and carers can participate. Third, we considered, 'Who are the participants?', and identified groups of people who are potentially excluded from participation processes. Fourth, we posed the question, 'Why is service user and carer participation important?', and identified the different mandates underpinning service user and carer involvement. Finally, we asked, 'What are the benefits of service user and carer participation?', both for service users, carers and service providers.

Whenever you are involved in service user and carer participation, ask yourself the following questions:

- What do I mean by service user and carer participation?

- What opportunities can I create in my practice to promote service user and carer participation?

- Why is this important?

- Who should I involve in this process? Are there any individuals or groups of people who have not been included and whose views are not represented?

- What can I learn from this process about myself and about other people?

It is important to bear in mind the following:

- know why you are involving service users and/or carers;

- know the reasons why your agency needs to involve service users and carers;

- be creative about finding ways to include service users and carers in all arenas and in all stages of social work practice;

- be aware of the power that you have as a social worker;

- try to ensure that everyone is included as much as they want to be;

- know the practical benefits of participation for service users, carers and services.

Carr, S (2004) *Has service user participation made a difference to social care services?* Position Paper No. 3. London: Social Care Institute for Excellence.

This report summarises the key themes and findings from the synthesis of six literature reviews on the impact of service user participation on change and improvement in social care services.

Heffernan, K (2006) Social work, new public management and the language of 'service user'. *British Journal of Social Work*, 36, (1), 139–147.

This article highlights the importance of language in social work, and explores the development of the term 'service user', arguing that it may be detrimental to those to whom it refers.

Kemshall, H and Littlechild, R (2000) *User involvement and participation in social care. Research informing practice*. London: Jessica Kingsley Publishers.

This book explores strategies for effectively involving users in the planning, delivery and evaluation of social work and social care services.

www.carersuk.org – Carers UK

This website provides information and advice to carers in England about their rights and how to get support. Links are given to relevant websites for carers living in Northern Ireland, Scotland and Wales.

www.carers.org – The Princess Royal Trust for Carers

This interactive website provides information and advice to carers across the UK. It also provides access to support for both adult and young carers.

www.shapingourlives.org.uk – Shaping Our Lives

This is the website of Shaping Our Lives, the national user-controlled network, which works with service users, carers and other key stakeholders to give service users more control and choice over the services that they use.

www.solnetwork.org.uk – Shaping Our Lives Networking Website

This innovative, service-user developed website resource provides a forum for service user-controlled organisations to voice their views and concerns, share information and support service user involvement at a national level as well as link with worldwide international user-controlled organisations. At the time of writing, it is planned to open the website up to non-service, non-user controlled organisations that have an interest in supporting the development of local user involvement aimed at delivering better service outcomes. These organisations will be able to use the website for disseminating work, consulting service users and other participatory purposes.

Chapter 2

Origins and development of service user and carer involvement and participation

This chapter will help you to meet the following National Occupational Standards:

Key Role 1: Prepare for, and work with individuals, families, carers, groups and communities to assess their needs and circumstances.
- Work with individuals, families, carers, groups and communities to help them make informed decisions.
- Assess needs and options to recommend a course of action.

Key Role 2: Plan, carry out, review and evaluate social work practice, with individuals, families, carers, groups, communities and other professionals.
- Respond to crisis situations.
- Interact with individuals, families, carers, groups and communities to achieve change and development and to improve life opportunities.
- Prepare, produce, implement and evaluate plans with individuals, families, carers, groups, communities and professional colleagues.
- Support the development of networks to meet assessed needs and planned outcomes.
- Work with groups to promote individual growth, development and independence.

Key Role 3: Support individuals to represent their needs, views and circumstances.
- Advocate with, and on behalf of, individuals, families, carers, groups and communities.
- Prepare for, and participate in decision-making forums.

Key Role 4: Manage risk to individuals, families, carers, groups, communities, self and colleagues.
- Assess and manage risks to individuals, families, carers, groups and communities.

Key Role 5: Manage and be accountable, with supervision and support, for your own social work practice within your organisation.
- Contribute to the management of resources and services.
- Manage, present and share records and reports.
- Work within multi-disciplinary and multi-organisational teams, networks and systems.

Key Role 6: Demonstrate professional competence in social work practice.
- Research, analyse, evaluate, and use current knowledge of best social work practice.
- Work within agreed standards of social work practice and ensure own professional development.
- Contribute to the promotion of best social work practice.

It will also introduce you to the following academic standards as set out in the social work subject benchmark statements:

3.1.1 Social work services and service users
- The nature of social work services in a diverse society.
- The relationship between agency policies, legal requirements and professional boundaries in shaping the nature of services provided in inter-disciplinary contexts and the issues associated with working across professional boundaries and within different disciplinary groups.

3.1.2 The service delivery context

- The location of contemporary social work within both historical and comparative perspectives, including European and international contexts.
- The complex relationships between public, social and political philosophies, policies and priorities and the organisation and practice of social work, including the contested nature of these.
- The issues and trends in modern public and social policy and their relationship to contemporary practice and service delivery in social work.
- The significance of legislative and legal frameworks and service delivery standards.
- The current range and appropriateness of statutory, voluntary and private agencies providing community-based, day-care, residential and other services and the organisational systems inherent within these.

3.1.3 Values and ethics

- The nature, historical evolution and application of social work values.
- The moral concepts of rights, responsibility, freedom, authority and power inherent in the practice of social workers as moral and statutory agents.
- The complex relationships between justice, care and control in social welfare and the practical and ethical implications of these.

3.1.4 Social work theory

- Research-based concepts and critical explanations from social work theory and other disciplines that contribute to the knowledge base of social work.
- The relevance of sociological perspectives to understanding societal and structural influences on human behaviour at individual, group and community levels.

3.1.5 The nature of social work practice

- The characteristics of practice in a range of community-based and organisational settings including group-care, within statutory, voluntary and private sectors, and the factors influencing changes in practice within these contexts.

The subject skills highlighted to demonstrate this knowledge in practice include:

3.2.2 Problem-solving skills

3.2.2.1 Managing problem-solving activities.

3.2.2.2 Gathering information.

3.2.2.3 Analysis and synthesis.

3.2.2.4 Intervention and evaluation.

3.2.3 Communication skills

- Listen actively to others, engage appropriately with the life experiences of service users, understand accurately their viewpoint and overcome personal prejudices to respond appropriately to a range of complex personal and interpersonal situations.

3.2.4 Skills in working with others

- Involve users of social work services in ways that increase their resources, capacity and power to influence factors affecting their lives.
- Consult actively with others, including service users, who hold relevant information or expertise.
- Act co-operatively with others, liaising and negotiating across differences such as organisational and professional boundaries and differences of identity or language.
- Develop effective helping relationships and partnerships with other individuals, groups and organisations that facilitate change.
- Act with others to increase social justice by identifying and responding to prejudice, institutional discrimination and structural inequality.
- Act within a framework of multiple accountability.
- Challenge others when necessary, in ways that are most likely to produce positive outcomes.

5.2.1 Knowledge and understanding

- Ability to use this knowledge and understanding in work within specific practice contexts.
- Recognition of the potential and limitations of social work as a practice based discipline.

Introduction

It has been acknowledged in recent years that despite its declared purpose, social work has not always operated with the interests of service users at its heart (see Cairney, Chettle, Clark, Davis, Gosling, Harvey, Jephcote, Labana, Lymbery, Pendred and Russell, 2006). Although founded on the principles of citizenship, compassion and social justice in support of those least powerful in society, the professionalisation of social work has, some would argue, resulted in worker–client relationships that are becoming increasingly char-acterised by control and supervision rather than care (Jones, Ferguson, Lavalette and Penketh, 2003/2007). In losing its focus on caring, social work has moved away from what matters to service users (Cairney *et al.*, 2006), does not always recognise or value equally the insights and experiences of its service users and their carers.

The literature on the development of service users' knowledge and theories endorses this view. Historically, service users' views, knowledge and expertise have been marginalised and invalidated (Beresford, 1997 and Croft and Beresford, 1998, both cited in Beresford, 2000, p495) on the basis of perceived:

- inability (people with disabilities and older people);

- unreliability, and illogicality of thought, perception and understanding (mental health system survivors);

- intellectual shortcomings (people with learning difficulties);

- unreliability, lack of knowledge and understanding, and incompetence (children, young people and older people);

(Beresford, 2000; Lansdown, 1994; Age Concern, 2005)

It is important, however, to acknowledge the one key quality that distinguishes service users', carers' and social workers' knowledge and perspectives – namely that service users' and carers' knowledge grows out of personal and collective experience of policy, practice and services (Beresford, 2000). It is service users and carers who are, after all, on the receiving end of social policy and social work provision. It is they who are best placed to identify what 'works' or doesn't 'work' and to contribute to shaping future service provi-sion. Social work, therefore, has much to learn from these movements if it is *to be defined not by its function for the state but by its value base* (Jones et al., 2007, p201).

Over the last two decades, service users' movements, such as the disability movement and the mental health system survivors' movement, have introduced innovatory and insightful ways of seeing, and responding to individual and social problems (Jones et al., 2007) – perhaps the most significant expression of this being the social model of disability devel-oped by the disabled people's movement. In promoting relevant, alternative approaches to working with service users' needs, these movements have developed and indeed, some-times forced their new knowledge onto professional, academic, political and policy-making agendas (Beresford, 2000).

In this chapter, we shall take an historical perspective, considering the origins of interest in service user and carer involvement. We shall trace the development of two specific service users' movements within the United Kingdom, together with the carers' movement and, where appropriate, make comparisons with international developments. In the second part of the chapter, we shall examine the legal and policy framework underpinning individual and collective involvement in social work practice, and explore the shifting emphases in policy development over the past two decades.

The origins of interest in service user and carer involvement

Service users and carers have always had perspectives about their direct experience of policy, practice and services, *from the earliest days of secular and religious charity and the beginnings of state intervention and the old Poor Law* (Beresford, 2000, p492). It is only within the past two decades, however, that service users and carers have become more visible and vocal within society, and made more of an impact on policy and practice. The government now actively seeks service user and carer views on national issues; service providers are required to consult and involve them in personal and agency decision-making processes, and educationalists are required to seek their help in providing professional training. So how has service user and carer involvement become *one of the guiding formal principles of social services*? (Beresford, 2000, p491)

Let us consider, for a moment, some of the different reasons for the growing interest in service user and carer involvement.

ACTIVITY 2.1

How do we explain the emergence of service user and carer involvement and participation in social work in the United Kingdom? Try to think of the possible factors that might explain this development.

Comment

Activity 2.1 may not have been as easy as it may have seemed at first sight. Indeed, you may have thought of only a few factors, but don't worry if this is the case. The origins and development of service user and carer involvement are, as we are beginning to see, complex, and relate to a number of social and political changes that have occurred, both nationally and internationally, during the past 60 years. These include the following.

- *The development of new philosophies* – the emergence of normalisation and social models of disability which emphasise people's rights and participation (Beresford, 1994).

- *The development of civil and welfare 'rights' movements* – the post-Second World War movement in the United States and Westernised industrialised countries towards increasing civil rights for disadvantaged groups (Campbell, 1996) and promoting citizenship which led, for example, to the emergence of the Gay Liberation, Black Civil Rights and the Disability Rights movements with their emphasis on enabling people to attain their full civil rights.

- *The lack of accountability of traditional welfare services* – public dissatisfaction with the poor quality, lack of responsiveness and lack of accountability of welfare and other public services (Beresford, 1994; Croft and Beresford, 1996).

- *The emergence of service users' and carers' movements* – the emergence of a wide range of groups of carers and service users who, dissatisfied with the welfare services and support received (Oliver, 1990; Beresford, 1994; Carers UK, 2002), demanded different, better and more responsive services.

- *The emergence of 'self-help' groups and organisations* – the growth of self-help as a concept, and the establishment of a range of self-help organisations, support groups and projects, based on the *therapeutic contribution of the non-expert, and the centrality of personal experience as a powerful tool for change* (Campbell, 1996, p221). These support services established different relationships with service users and met needs that had been ignored previously (Croft and Beresford, 1996).

- *The development of more collaborative ways of working* – seeking to alter the balance of power between service users and social workers, progressive welfare professionals promoted ways of working that were based on the principles of equality and partnership (Beresford, 1994).

- *The disenchantment with the British post-war welfare state* – the political right of the 1970s perceived the 'nanny' welfare state as creating and perpetuating dependency, and objected to government intervention, preferring a greater role for the private market (Croft and Beresford, 1996).

- *The consumerism of the 1980s* – emphasis was placed on 'mixed economy' approaches to public and welfare services, and the principles of commercial consumerism (accessibility, information, choice, redress and representation) (Braye, 2000).

- *The influence of international service user and survivor movements* – ideas and examples from other countries, such as the USA, with its strong civil rights tradition (Oliver, 1990; Barnes, 2000), and the Netherlands, influenced developments in the UK (Campbell, 1996). For example, the development of Patients' Councils and advocacy in psychiatric units was influenced by activities undertaken in the Netherlands (Campbell, 1996).

- *Poverty and social exclusion* – the impact of the Thatcher government's commitment to reducing public expenditure, minimising the role of the state and privatising services, on disadvantaged groups such as those with disabilities (Oliver, 1990).

As we have seen from this activity, present-day service user involvement in social work practice cannot be considered in isolation. It needs to be understood within the much broader context of the social, cultural, economic and political changes that have impacted on the United Kingdom, mainland Europe and North America over the past 60 years. In particular, the origins and development of service user participation need to be understood within the context of the development of movements of health and social care service users and their carers, to which we will now turn our attention.

The emergence of service users' and carers' movements

Although little research has been published on the history of the service users' and carers' movements in the United Kingdom, service users, carers and their organisations have recently started to produce their own histories in professional publications, mainstream print and on their own websites (see, for example, Campbell, 1996, 2006; Dybwad and Bersani, 1996; Carers UK, 2002). The benefits of such histories are fourfold. First, these social histories document the increasing significance of the service users' and carers' movements in public, political, policy and professional debate over the last 60 years, highlighting their increasing strength and influence at local, national and international levels. Second, they chart the social, political and economic changes that have resulted from the activities of various service users' and carers' movements, and the ways in which these activities have helped to change public opinion and behaviour towards groups of service users and carers over time. Third, these histories provide clues about the types of problems and conflicts that have been experienced within the various movements, and the challenges that may still need to be addressed in the future. An example of this is the ongoing struggle that exists within some organisations about how service user and carer issues are voiced; that is, who should speak for service users and carers? Should this be the staff from organisations that have traditionally worked on behalf of those groups named in their titles, or representatives of newer, more democratic organisations controlled and run by the people themselves? Finally, the histories of the service users' and carers' movements also highlight, for us, some of the driving forces behind the government's more recent concern with issues of user involvement and participation, particularly within social work practice and education.

As you are already aware from Chapter 1, the service users' and carers' movements are not a homogenous group of people. Clear distinctions exist both within and between the different movements with regard to their ways of working, their philosophies and their objectives. Whilst the disabled people's movement is considered to be the most strongly established and visible of all of the service users' movements (Beresford, 2000), there has been a strong collective response from people included in other social care categories, including people with learning difficulties, older people, psychiatric survivors, and people living with HIV/AIDS, drug or alcohol dependence. Let us then for a moment consider the origins and development of three different movements of health and social care service users and their carers.

The Appendix at the end of this book presents a timeline comparing the origins, development and achievements of three different movements: the disabled people's movement, the mental health system survivors' movement and the adult carers' movement. In selecting these movements for discussion, it is not intended to divert attention from the histories of other service user or carer movements such as the movements of people with learning difficulties, older people or young carers. You may like to chart the origins and development of some of these or other health and social care service user movements yourself, using the resources listed at the end of this chapter.

ACTIVITY 2.2

Read through the Appendix outlining the historical development of the carers' movement and two service users' movements in the UK. As you do so, note down any trends, patterns or interesting points that you notice.

Comment

When considering the development of the different service users' and carers' movements, you may have noted the following.

- The rapid growth and development of these movements over the past 20 years, and the comparative speed with which ideas about user and carer participation have gained official approval (Campbell, 1996).

- The wide range of roles and activities undertaken by each movement, including consultation and advice on service provision and practice; creation and provision of services including self-help and support groups; establishment of individual and collective advocacy schemes; consciousness-raising, educating, and challenging public and media misconceptions; campaigning, parliamentary lobbying and research.

- Movements may be started by individuals but individuals cannot represent a movement – there is a need for a collective policy-making process whereby the emphasis shifts from the individual to collective action. Establishing a coherent position on issues is important.

- The diverse emphases placed by the different service users' and carers' movements over time. For example, the focus by the disabled people's movement on campaigning for anti-discrimination legislation; the mental health service user movements' focus on improving the nature of services and promoting new understandings of mental illness in order to reduce public fear; the work undertaken by the carers' movement in improving the recognition of, and financial support to carers.

- The significance, over time, of renaming organisations or networks as a way of embracing new identities, new perspectives, new positions and new aspirations for the future.

- The impact of one movement on another, giving greater force and focus to ideas of involvement. For example, although the position and rights of service users and carers have not always been seen as complementary, the *language and logic* of carer involvement have been directly informed by user involvement ideas and the service user movement, in particular, the disabled people's movement (Roulstone, Hudson, Kearney and Martin with Warren, 2006, p5).

- The impact of service user and carer campaigning on the existing legislative programme of government. For example, the carers' movement's success in securing legal rights for carers (Carers (Recognition and Services) Act 1995 and Carers and Disabled Children Act 2000) and in tackling the barriers that carers face in accessing employment, education and leisure (Carers (Equal Opportunities) Act 2005). Also, the disabled people's movement's success in converting all of the political parties and the vast majority of voluntary organisations to the idea of legislation to outlaw discrimination (Disability Discrimination Acts 1995 and 2005), and in producing new legislation to promote independent living through direct payments (Community Care (Direct Payments) Act 1996).

Charting the origins and development of movements of health and social care service users and their carers, therefore, helps to highlight the ways in which these movements

> *have been associated with major changes in legislation, policy, culture, theory and provision, all of which have impacted upon the policy, provision and practice of social work.*

> (Beresford and Croft, 2004, p62)

The legislative and policy framework

Developing the participation of service users and carers in the services that they receive from health, social care or education providers is no longer an optional 'bolt-on extra' for professionals – it is central to the current government legislative, policy and guidance framework underpinning the delivery of public services. In short, participation is now a legal requirement that all professionals working in social work and social care must address.

The legislative and policy framework is, however, highly complex. Tables 2.1, 2.2 and 2.3 present a chronology and guide to the key pieces of legislation, policy guidance, practice guidance and service standards providing for the involvement and participation of children, young people, adult service users and their carers in the development of health and social services in England. Starting with relevant law and policy initiatives from the end of the 1980s, we follow these developments through to the present day.

Table 2.1 Key legislation and policy relevant to the participation of adults and children

Specific legislation, policy and practice guidance	Main provisions in respect of adults' and children's participation
Modernising Social Services (DoH, 1998c)	Outlined government's new vision to put users at the heart of social services. Annual user satisfaction surveys to be carried out by local authorities.
Human Rights Act 1998	Provided for individual protection of ECHR (European Convention on Human Rights) rights through UK courts. Has the potential to empower service users to challenge agency and professional decisions made without their participation (Braye, 2000).
Local Government Act 1999	Placed duty on local authorities to carry out best value reviews of all their services (s5). Requirement to prepare annual best value performance plans that incorporate the wishes and priorities of local people, including children and young people (s6).
Care Standards Act 2000	Provided for the publication of National Minimum Standards for care services (s23) to ensure the protection of vulnerable service users, to drive up the quality of care, and to increase service user participation by encouraging choice and independence. The Act also provided for the creation of a Children's Rights Director to protect the rights of children living away from home (Sch 1(10)).
Health and Social Care Act 2001	Placed a duty on health authorities, primary care trusts and NHS trusts to involve and consult patients and the public in the planning of service provision, the development and consideration of proposals for change and decisions about the operation of services (s11). Ensured provision of independent advocacy services for people making or intending to make a complaint (s12).
Disability Discrimination Act 2005	Duty placed on public authorities to promote equality of opportunity between disabled people and others, and to encourage participation by disabled people in public life (s3).
Improving the Life Chances of Disabled People (PMSU, DfWP, DoH, DfES, ODPM, 2005)	Outlined government's new vision that by 2025, disabled people should have full opportunities and choices to improve their quality of life, and be respected and included as equal members of society.

37

Specific legislation, policy and practice guidance	Main provisions in respect of adult and children's participation
Policy applicable to carers	
Carers (Recognition and Services) Act 1995	Carers given rights to an assessment of their ability to provide and to continue to provide care, and for the local authority to take into account the results of that assessment when making decisions about the provision of services to the person with care needs (s1).
National Strategy for Carers (DoH, 1999a)	Placed emphasis on individual carers being involved and consulted about the services that they need. All services used by carers should involve them in service planning and provide a forum in which consultation about service provision can take place.
Carers and Disabled Children Act 2000	Extended the inclusion and participation of carers by affording them rights to packages of assessed support even when the person they provide care to has refused an assessment (Roulstone *et al.*, 2006) or provision of services (s2).
Community Care (Delayed Discharges) Act 2003	Carers given new rights to services before a patient is discharged from hospital (s4).
Carers (Equal Opportunities) Act 2004	Duty placed on local authorities to inform carers of their right to assessment (s1), which should include consideration of their leisure, training and work, or wish to work (s2).

Table 2.2 Legislation and policy most relevant to the participation of adults

Specific legislation, policy and practice guidance	Main provisions in respect of adult participation
National Health Services and Community Care Act 1990	Local authority duty to assess an individual's needs for community care services (s47(1)); to consult with stakeholders regarding the publication of plans for the provision of community care services in their area (s46(1)) and to consult with voluntary organisations who appear to represent the interests of service users, potential service users or their carers (s46(2)(d)).
Community Care in the Next Decade and Beyond (DoH, 1990)	Promoted the involvement of service users and carers in the assessment and care management process. Emphasis placed on community care plans and consumer choice.
Care Management and Assessment: Summary of Practice Guidance (DoH and SSI, 1991a)	Service user involvement and empowerment presented as a central rationale for change in social care.
Framework for Local Community Care Charters (DoH, 1994)	Emphasis placed on local authorities consulting service users, carers and others to ensure that their charters reflect local priorities and concerns.
Consultation Counts: Guidelines (DoH, 1996a)	Emphasis placed on consultation being a continuous dialogue, that seeks service user and carer views and advice locally to influence change and development, not a once-a-year public relations exercise.
Community Care (Direct Payments) Act 1996	Service users afforded the right to opt to commission services and to receive payment for services direct from the local authority (Johns, 2005).
Better Care, Higher Standards (DoH, 1999e)	Promoted the involvement of service users and carers in developing joint local charters with a local authority and in individual decision-making processes regarding long-term care arrangements or support.

Specific legislation, policy and practice guidance	Main provisions in respect of adult participation
National Service Framework for Mental Health (DoH, 1999d)	Promoted the social inclusion of people with mental health problems and service user and carer involvement in the planning and delivery of multi-disciplinary care services.
Valuing People (DoH, 2001a)	Promoted the active involvement of people with learning difficulties and their carers in decision-making processes that affect their lives; planning, monitoring and reviewing services, evaluating the quality of services and policy development at local and national levels.
National Service Framework for Older People (DoH, 2001b)	Promoted the person-centred approach providing for the active involvement of older people in decision-making processes about their own needs and care (Standard 2). Also promoted the involvement of older people and their carers in the planning and development of local health and social care services.
Single Assessment Process Guidance for Local Implementation (DoH, 2002a)	Acknowledged service users' expertise and placed older people's perspectives, views and wishes at the centre of assessment and care planning processes.

Table 2.3 Legislation and policy most relevant to the participation of children and young people

Specific legislation, policy and practice guidance	Main provisions in respect of children's participation
Children Act 1989	A court must have regard to a child's ascertainable wishes and feelings (considered in the light of the child's age and understanding) when considering the child's welfare (s1(3)(a)). Duty placed on local authorities to ascertain the wishes and feelings of a child they look after or propose to look after before making any decisions (s22(4)).
UN Convention on the Rights of the Child 1989	Ratified by the UK government in 1991, Article 12 emphasises the right of children to express their views and to have them taken into account in any matters affecting them.
Children's Services Planning Guidance LAC (96) 10 (DoH, 1996b)	Emphasis placed on service users as partners in the planning process, not passive recipients; consultation being an integral and continuing part of the process, and service users having a role in monitoring services and providing feedback.
When Leaving Home is also Leaving Care (DoH and SSI, 1997)	Emphasis placed on consulting young people individually about their wishes and feelings and involving them in discussions and plans about their future; consulting them about the services provided.
Quality Protects (DoH, 1998a)	Emphasis placed on local authorities listening to, and involving children and young people in policy and service development, and in individual care planning.
Government's Objectives for Children's Social Services, (DoH, 1999c)	Promoted the active involvement of users and carers in planning services and in tailoring individual packages of care; effective mechanisms to be put in place to handle complaints (Objective 8). Local authorities required to demonstrate that children and young people are becoming more satisfied with services (Sub-objective 8.2).

Specific legislation, policy and practice guidance	Main provisions in respect of children's participation
National Standards for Foster Care (DoH, 1999b)	The standards support looked-after children's and young people's rights to participate and contribute to decision-making in individual care planning, case recording, recruitment and review of foster carers, development of policy and procedures, and making complaints and representation about their care.
Working Together to Safeguard Children (DoH, HO and DfEE, 1999)	Placed emphasis on basic safeguards for children living away from home including access to independent advocacy services and effective, accessible complaints procedures.
Framework for the Assessment of Children in Need and their Families, (DoH, 2000a)	Placed emphasis on direct work with children during assessment using multiple age, gender, and culturally appropriate methods for ascertaining their wishes and feelings.
Learning to Listen: Core Principles (CYPU, 2001)	Core principles for children's and young people's participation in the planning, delivery and evaluation of government policies and services.
Adoption and Children Act 2002	Courts and adoption agencies to have regard to the child's ascertainable wishes and feelings when making decisions about an adoption (considered in the light of the child's age and understanding) (s1(4)(a)); Local authorities to provide advocacy services to looked-after children and care leavers who make or intend to make representation (including a complaint) (s119).
Listening, Hearing and Responding (DoH, 2002c)	Department of Health action plan to promote children's and young people's participation in decision-making processes.
National Standards for the Provision of Children's Advocacy Services (DoH, 2002d)	Advocacy should be led by the views and wishes of children and young people (Standard 1) and should listen to these views and ideas in order to improve the service provided (Standard 8). Advocacy services should have an effective and easy to use complaints procedure (Standard 9).
Every Child Matters (DfES, 2003)	Outlined government's commitment to providing more opportunities for children and young people to get involved in the planning, delivery and evaluation of policies and services at a local and national level.
Children Act 2004	Local authority duty to ascertain and give due consideration (having regard to age and understanding) to a child's wishes and feelings regarding the provision of services for a child in need; and action to be taken during a child protection enquiry under s 47(5)(a) of Children Act 1989 (s53); children's services authority required to prepare and publish a children and young people's plan (s 17).
National Service Framework for Children, Children, Young people and Maternity Services (DoH, 2004)	young people and families should receive high quality services, which are co-ordinated around their individual and family needs and take account of their views (Standard 3).
Children and Young People's Plan (England) Regulations 2005	Local authorities must consult with local children, young people and others during the preparation of Children and Young People's Plans.
Child Care Act 2006	In discharging their duties in relation to early childhood services, an English local authority must have regard to information available about the views of young children (s3(5)).

Specific legislation, policy and practice guidance	Main provisions in respect of children's participation
Working Together to Safeguard Children (HM Government, 2006)	All organisations that provide services for, or work with, children must have a culture of listening to, and engaging in dialogue with, children. This means seeking children's views in ways that are appropriate for their age and understanding, and taking account of those views in decision-making processes and in the establishment or development of services. All training in safeguarding and promoting the welfare of children should create an ethos that is child-centred and promotes the participation of children and families in the process.

The tables provide a useful overview of the growing shift in legislation and policy informing the development of service user and carer involvement and participation in social work practice over the past two decades. As can be seen, there are dozens of policies and a number of pieces of legislation that are relevant to the involvement of service users and their carers. Although initially slow to develop, many of the most pertinent policies and pieces of legislation have been generated during the past decade in response to New Labour's public service 'modernisation' agenda. These developments reflect, in part, the growing understanding of and insight into both the nature of service user and carer perspectives and personal experiences that have resulted from the activities of the various service user and carer movements, and the increasing value that has been placed by government on harnessing this expertise to improve the quality of existing public services.

Whilst policies create the framework for involvement and participation in social work practice, legislation provides the legal mandate which confers specific 'rights' to involvement. As can be seen in the tables, service users' and carers' rights to participation are enshrined in a range of child welfare and adult legislation. The participation of carers in the design, review and delivery of services, for example, is now a key statutory requirement with substantive rights attached (Roulstone et al., 2006). You may have noticed in Table 2.1 that the Carers (Recognition and Services) Act 1995 gave carers access to an assessment, whilst the Carers and Disabled Children Act 2000 further extended the inclusion and participation of carers by affording them rights to packages of assessed support even when the person they provide care to has refused an assessment (Roulstone *et al.*, 2006) for community care services or refused the provision of services.

In practice, the legislative and policy framework governing the involvement and participation of service users and carers in social work practice is complex, which has led to difficulties for professionals, particularly in the 1990s, with regard to interpretation and implementation. Although the concept of service user and carer involvement was not initiated by the 1990 NHS and Community Care Act or the 1989 Children Act, what these two pieces of legislation did was to make consultation with service users a legislative duty for local authorities and in so doing, ensured that the principle of involvement became integral to the legal framework for social care services (Braye, 2000). The statutory guidance accompanying both these acts is, as Braye remarks:

> *peppered with references to the need to inform, consult and involve people who use services.*

(Braye, 2000, p13)

In tracing the development of policy underpinning service user and carer involvement and participation, we can see, however, that earlier documents placed emphasis on the concepts of 'consultation' and 'involvement', without any clear definition of their meaning. This proved problematic for professionals and led to difficulties in interpreting and implementing law and policy. In children's services, for example, research focusing on the implementation in practice of the Children Act 1989 found that the process of children's participation was not as child-centred as it should be, due in part to the apparent lack of clarity among professionals about the meaning of the term 'consultation' (Aldgate and Statham, 2001). Clear and accessible information, talking over anxieties and giving children opportunities to influence plans, it was argued, played an important part in consultation, thereby enabling children and young people to make informed choices and decisions (Aldgate and Statham, 2001).

A further tension during the 1990s was created by the challenge to establish new patterns of service delivery that were no longer provider-dominated ('supply-led' services) but purchaser-dominated ('needs-led' services). For change to be effective, the consultation and involvement of service users and carers in planning and providing for community care required that professional agencies engage in a major culture change. Valuing the perspectives of service users and carers, however, challenged the traditional service-led culture of social service departments, resulting in many departments resisting change (Audit Commission, 1992). In consequence, many groups of service users and carers continued to be marginalised from consultation and planning processes. In children's services, for example, despite various initiatives to promote parental involvement in case conferences, little changed with regard to children's participation (Thoburn, Lewis and Shemmings, 1995, cited in Braye, 2000, p15). Similarly, in provision for adults, attention was drawn to the gaps in communication between local authorities and service users which necessitated the use of independent advocacy and mediation services to obtain minimum information about access to community care services (Coombs and Sedgewick, 1998, cited in Braye, 2000, p14). In consequence, existing legal mandates for participation and involvement were criticised as ineffectual (Braye, 2000). Participation required that service users and carers take much more of an active part in influencing decision-making, and in influencing the direction and implementation of change. Increased requirements for more active service user and carer participation in service development and regulation subsequently became set out in government directives on Best Value for Local Authorities (Local Government Act 1999), and in the legislation and policy guidance associated with the Government's modernisation agenda (Carr, 2004). As can be seen from Tables 2.1–2.3, these documents placed greater emphasis on the active participation of service users and carers in the planning, delivery and evaluation of services, and in the development of government policies, which impacted directly on their future lives.

As shown in the Appendix, the service user and carer lobbies played a much more influential role in shaping policy and legislation from the 1990s onwards, as policy-making began to develop through a process of debate, negotiation and adjustment. In consequence, legislation and policy have contained strong elements of incrementalism, in which compromises have had to be reached (Aldridge and Becker, 2003). The 'tie in' requiring that carers' assessments under the Carers (Recognition and Services) Act 1995 be linked to service users' assessments, for example, is just one of the compromises that arose from this type of negotiated process (Aldridge and Becker, 2003). Subsequent legislation extended carers' rights to an independent assessment (Carers and Disabled Children Act 2000) and placed a duty on local authorities to inform carers of their rights to an assessment (Carers (Equal Opportunities) Act 2004).

The Better Government for Older People (BGOP) initiative, launched in 1998 as a two-year programme, however, represented a significant step forward in policy development, by engaging older people as citizens in developing ways of reshaping public services for the needs of the future (Janzon and Law, 2003). Based on the principles of partnership, the programme brought together older people and their organisations, national and local government, service providers and academics. The recommendations from this programme helped to shape future policy development and service delivery by, for example, committing the government to act to combat age discrimination and promoting better engagement with older people in the planning and decision-making processes that affect their lives. Significantly, the National Service Framework for Older People (DoH, 2001b) included a strong requirement that older people be involved as *partners* in the development process, rather than simply being *consulted* (Janzon and Law, 2003). Subsequently, older people have been involved in all the implementation stages of the National Services Framework, working, in particular, through local implementation teams to put plans for improvement into action. Central to these plans has been the need to involve older people as genuine partners. Such inclusion and involvement of service users through all stages of the process is a welcome development. It provides opportunities for true engagement and has the potential to deliver real change.

ACTIVITY **2.3**

Read the case study below. Using your knowledge of the legislative and policy framework underpinning service user and carer involvement discussed in this chapter, think about how a social worker's approach to involving this family in decision-making processes might differ today from that in 1994. Identify legislation and policy informing the involvement of Sharon and Peter, indicating the nature of the involvement provided for.

	Sharon		Peter	
	Legislation and policy	*Nature of involvement*	*Legislation and policy*	*Nature of involvement*
1994				
today				

Case Scenario

Peter is 16 years old. He has learning difficulties and is undertaking a general course at a local college of further education. He cares for his mum, Sharon, who has lupus, a very painful and disabling condition that reduces her immune system and affects her mobility. Sharon's social worker left the area 18 months ago, and there has been no review of her care package during this time. Her condition has been deteriorating for some time, and her awareness of this and her fears for the future are impacting on her mental health. Peter's caring tasks vary according to his mum's condition and other levels of formal home care support. Over the past 18 months, he has taken increasing responsibility for major household tasks including cooking meals, cleaning and gardening. He regularly looks after his three-year-old sister when his mother needs a rest, and generally keeps an eye on his mum to make sure that she is alright. Peter feels under considerable stress and is considering giving up his college course.

Comment

This activity will help to consolidate the knowledge base covered in this chapter. We have not provided examples of what you may identify here as this gives you an opportunity to check through your understanding of this chapter.

C H A P T E R   S U M M A R Y

In this chapter, we have traced the origins and development of service user and carer involvement and participation in social work, paying particular attention to the increasing significance of the service users' and carers' movements in public, political, policy and professional debate. We have explored some of the different reasons for the growing interest in service user and carer involvement, and have seen that these developments need to be understood within the much broader context of the social, cultural, economic and political changes impacting on the United Kingdom, mainland Europe and North America during the past 60 years.

This chapter has also charted the development of movements of health and social care service users and their carers, and has highlighted the ways in which these movements have been associated with major changes in legislation, policy, culture, theory and social work provision.

We have also explored the legislative and policy framework underpinning service user and carer participation in social work practice, and traced the shifts in policy development that have occurred over the past two decades. Although initially slow to develop, many of the most pertinent policies and pieces of legislation have been generated during the past decade in response to New Labour's public service 'modernisation' agenda. In the struggle towards empowerment of service user and carers, the government has undertaken to provide a legal and policy framework that requires more active user and carer participation in service regulation and development. As we have seen, service users and carers, therefore, need to be involved as *partners*, rather than simply being *consulted* (Janzon and Law, 2003) about service delivery and developmental processes.

In the next chapter, we move on to consider some of the characteristics and features of participatory practice, identifying different levels of service user and carer participation, and some of the barriers that prevent the development of participatory practices.

FURTHER READING

Barnes, C and Mercer, G (2006) *Independent futures: Creating user-led disability services in a disabling society.* Bristol: The Policy Press.

This book provides a comprehensive review and analysis of the development and organisation of disability-related user-controlled services in the United Kingdom.

Becker, S, Aldridge, J and Dearden, C (1998) *Young carers and their families.* Oxford: Blackwell Science.

The first comprehensive publication to explore the development of awareness about the needs and rights of young carers.

Campbell, P (2006) *Some things you should know about user/survivor action: a Mind resource pack.* London: Mind.

A useful pack explaining how and why the service user movement developed, what activists have been fighting for, what action they have taken and what the movement has achieved.

Dybwad, G and Bersani, H (eds) (1996) *New voices: Self-advocacy by people with disabilities.* Cambridge, Massachusetts: Brookline Books.

A collection of papers, many written by self-advocates themselves, which provide an historical account of the self-advocacy movement across the Western world (USA, UK, Canada, Denmark and Australia), and examine the status of self-advocacy activities in each of these countries.

Older People's Steering Group (2004) *Older people shaping policy and practice*. York: Joseph Rowntree Foundation.

A report on a research programme examining the priorities that older people themselves defined as important for living well in later life.

Tilley, L (2004) *The history of self-advocacy for people with learning difficulties: International comparisons.* **www.open.ac.uk/hsc/ldsite/pdfs/tilleyconfrep04.pdf**

A useful report of an international conference held at the Open University to provide self-advocates, supporters and academics with an opportunity to explore how self-advocacy has developed historically within an international context.

www.ageconcern.org.uk – Age Concern

Age concern is a UK charity working with and for older people. This website provides up-to-date information on the organisation's campaigning activities and enables access to information on a range of topics including care, health, housing, income and pensions, leisure, travel, work and learning.

www.bgop.org.uk – Better Government for Older People

This website provides up-to-date information about developments across the UK and enables access to relevant publications and briefings.

www.cpa.org.uk – Centre for Policy on Ageing

The Centre for Policy and Ageing is an independent centre of research and reference which focuses on the wide-ranging needs of older people.

www.helptheaged.org.uk – Help the Aged

Help the Aged is a charity that is fighting to free older people in the UK and overseas from poverty, isolation, neglect, ageism and future deprivation.

www.mencap.org.uk – Mencap

Mencap is a voluntary organisation providing advice, information and support for people with learning difficulties, their families and carers.

www.mdx.ac.uk/www.study/mhtim.htm – *Mental health and learning disability history timeline*

This University of Middlesex resource by Andrew Roberts provides a useful timeline charting the history of policy and care for people with a mental illness and/or learning disability. A service users' history group timeline runs parallel to the main timeline. This can be found at **www.mdx.ac.uk/www.study/MPU.htm**

Chapter 3

Service user and carer involvement and participation: rhetoric or reality?

A C H I E V I N G   A   S O C I A L   W O R K   D E G R E E

This chapter will help you to meet the following National Occupational Standards:

Key Role 1: Prepare for, and work with individuals, families, carers, groups and communities to assess their needs and circumstances.

- Work with individuals, families, carers, groups and communities to help them make informed decisions.
- Assess needs and options to recommend a course of action.

Key Role 2: Plan, carry out, review and evaluate social work practice, with individuals, families, carers, groups, communities and other professionals.

- Interact with individuals, families, carers, groups and communities to achieve change and development and to improve life opportunities.
- Prepare, produce, implement and evaluate plans with individuals, families, carers, groups, communities and professional colleagues.

Key Role 3: Support individuals to represent their needs, views and circumstances.

- Advocate with, and on behalf of, individuals, families, carers, groups and communities.
- Prepare for, and participate in decision-making forums.

It will also introduce you to the following academic standards as set out in the social work subject benchmark statements:

3.1.1 Social work services and service users
- The nature of social work services in a diverse society.

3.1.2 The service delivery context
- The issues and trends in modern public and social policy and their relationship to contemporary practice and service delivery in social work.

3.1.3 Values and ethics
- The nature, historical evolution and application of social work values.
- The moral concepts of rights, responsibility, freedom, authority and power inherent in the practice of social workers as moral and statutory agents.

3.1.5 The nature of social work practice
- The characteristics of practice in a range of community-based and organisational settings including group-care, within statutory, voluntary and private sectors, and the factors influencing changes in practice within these contexts.
- The integration of theoretical perspectives and evidence from international research into the design and implementation of effective social work intervention with a wide range of service users, carers and others.

The subject skills highlighted to demonstrate this knowledge in practice include

3.2.2 Problem-solving skills

3.2.2.1 Managing problem-solving activities.

3.2.2.2 Gathering information.

3.2.2.3 Analysis and synthesis.

3.2.2.4 Intervention and evaluation.

3.2.3 Communication skills

- Listen actively to others, engage appropriately with the life experiences of service users, understand accurately their viewpoint and overcome personal prejudices to respond appropriately to a range of complex personal and interpersonal situations.

3.2.4 Skills in working with others

- Involve users of social work services in ways that increase their resources, capacity and power to influence factors affecting their lives.
- Consult actively with others, including service users, who hold relevant information or expertise.
- Develop effective helping relationships and partnerships with other individuals, groups and organisations that facilitate change.

Introduction

In tracing the origins of service user and carer involvement in social work practice, we saw how generalised initial guidance from the Department of Health has been. Much policy and practice guidance has served to reinforce the need to involve service users and carers both in negotiations about their individual care, and in the planning and management of services. In consequence, different approaches and models have been adopted in practice, as professionals have sought to develop involvement structures and strategies that are more meaningful to service users and carers. In the first part of this chapter, we examine some different approaches to participation and, using a range of models, explore the varying degrees or levels of participation and power afforded to service users and carers in practice.

In tracing the legislative and policy framework underpinning service user and carer involvement, and the growth and development of the service user and carer movements, we noted in Chapter 2 the wealth of opportunity that exists for promoting participation in social work. In the light of these developments, however, you may be wondering why greater progress has not been made. In the second part of this chapter, we examine some of the barriers or challenges to service user and carer participation, and consider some of the key characteristics of effective participatory practice. We also consider what needs to change organisationally for participation to become meaningful, and reflect upon the role that we all need to play in changing our organisations.

Approaches to service user and carer involvement

Two broad approaches to service user and carer involvement underpin social work practice:

- the *consumerist approach*, which is concerned with increasing the amount of choice that service users and carers exercise in the services that they use;

- the *democratic approach*, which focuses on the achievement of full and equal citizenship for service users and carers.

(Beresford and Croft, 1993)

The first of these models of involvement has been based on a market approach, in which increased competition between service providers results in the provision of more responsive services in order to gain the custom of service users. In this approach, professionals provide information that enables service users and carers to make informed choices, thereby influencing their individual consumption of services. In contrast, the democratic approach to participation places emphasis on people's participatory rights, the redistribution of power, and the achievement of full and equal citizenship, so that service users and carers gain more influence and control in the decision-making processes that affect them. In this approach, service users and carers may be involved in decision-making processes that focus on, for example, policy development, resource allocation, and the operational and strategic management of services, thereby helping to shape and influence their collective use of services. In Chapter 2, we saw that the democratic approach is one that has been adopted by service user-led organisations and campaigners such as Shaping Our Lives.

The approach adopted by welfare agencies has implications for the amount and type of involvement that service users and carers can have in decision-making processes. However, as Braye (2000) points out, whilst these models of participation appear conceptually distinct and at a theoretical level diametrically opposed, in practice, they can operate side by side. You may have observed, for example, how people with very different perspectives can work together on projects to improve participation. You may have also noticed, however, that as Braye suggests

> the consumerist model often has a stronger presence - it is more tangible and may appear easier to achieve - thus giving the illusion of participation without the substance.

(Braye, 2000, p19)

Levels of involvement and participation

The level and nature of engagement by service users and carers in decision-making processes about their own lives, as well as collective involvement in matters that affect them, varies greatly. Participation and involvement can mean *taking part in or being present at or it can mean knowing that one's actions and views are being noted and may be acted upon* (Sinclair and Franklin, 2000, p2). The following activity will help you to begin to explore a range of participatory opportunities, each reflecting different levels of service user or carer involvement.

ACTIVITY **3.1**

Think about the kinds of decisions that service users and carers can make about their own lives, and about policy and service development.

Now look at the scenarios below and decide whether they are examples of service users and carers:

- *taking control of the decisions that affect them;*
- *meaningfully participating as partners in decision-making;*

ACTIVITY **3.1** *continued*

- *extending influence over the decision-making processes;*

- *being consulted about decisions;*

- *merely being asked for or given information.*

Scenarios

1. *John, a 30-year-old male with learning difficulties, is invited to his individual pro-gramme planning meeting and after 30 minutes is asked if he has anything to say.*

2. *A group of service users with long-term conditions is asked to complete a survey about personal and home care services. As a result, a new policy is drafted and shown to them to check that their concerns have been addressed.*

3. *A group of looked-after children decide to raise money to purchase some gym equip-ment. They agree a strategy for raising the money, organise fundraising events and use the money raised to purchase the equipment.*

4. *A group of residents in a care home is involved in short-listing and interviewing for a new member of staff.*

5. *Tom has Parkinson's disease and is cared for full-time by his wife, Claire. Over the past year, Claire has represented her carers' group on the University Social Work Programme Advisory Committee, and has been paid as a guest lecturer to deliver training sessions about carers' issues to students on the programme.*

Comment

Thinking about different levels of participation makes us look at the way that we perceive and treat service users and carers. In the first scenario, you may have felt that John was asked for his views and opinions (giving information). However, no effort appears to have been made to include him in discussions about his own care at the start of the individual programme planning meeting or to explain to him how, and if, his views will affect the decision-making process. In the second scenario, a group of services users with long-term conditions is asked for their views on local personal and home care services (consultation), and their opinions are taken seriously. It is important to note here, however, that the survey has been designed and run by service providers. In contrast, in scenario 3 the idea and the implementation of the idea come from the children and young people themselves (control). In scenario 4, we can see that this group of residents is fully involved in decision-making processes that affect their home, with each party having an equal say in recruitment and selection (partnership). Similarly, in scenario 5 we see a genuine partner-ship between carers and university lecturing staff through Claire's representation on the advisory group and contribution to teaching activities.

What you may have noticed from this activity is that the different levels of involvement and participation are characterised by varying degrees of power sharing or equality (Braye, 2000) between the parties in the scenario. The issue of how much power service users and carers have in different decision-making processes is important. In full participation, power is shared equally (Pateman, 1970, cited in Braye, 2000, p20) between professionals, services users and carers, so that service users and carers are able to influence decision-making processes and shape the direction of change within an organisation or service area. To effect full and genuine participation, therefore, practitioners need to think carefully about their decision-making processes and the balance of power that exists between themselves and service users and carers.

The extent to which service users and carers are involved or participate in decision-making processes that affect their lives has been portrayed, traditionally, as a hierarchical process where the level and nature of participation varies according to the degree of power that an individual holds. Arnstein's 1969 model of a 'ladder of participation' outlines eight stages in ascending order of power sharing, from non-participation (manipulation and therapy), through levels of tokenism (informing, consultation and placation), to levels of citizen power (partnership, delegated power and citizen control) (Roulstone et al., 2006). Other typologies of participation have been adapted from this model. For example, Hart (1997) used the ladder metaphor to examine participatory initiatives involving children and young people. This model has been useful in enabling social workers to consider whether, for example, looked-after children's involvement in decision-making processes is tokenistic. Hoyes et al. (1993) also based their 'ladder of empowerment' on Arnstein's model, providing a way of assessing the extent to which service users are genuinely empowered under community care arrangements (cited in Nocon and Qureshi, 1998, p50).

All of the above models highlight the need to understand and distinguish different levels of participation and power afforded to service users and carers within organisations. Where these models are less helpful, however, is in depicting participation as a hierarchy in which the main aim is to reach the top of the ladder. Different levels of participation may be appropriate for different individuals and groups of service users and carers at different times and in different contexts (Kirby, Lanyon, Cronin and Sinclair, 2003b). Kirby et al. (2003b) suggest that levels of participation are determined by:

- the context;
- the task;
- the decisions being made;
- an individual's abilities, interests and availability;
- the culture of participation present within an organisation.

Figure 3.1 shows a non-hierarchical, holistic model of service user and carer involvement, which places service users and carers at the centre of a range of decision-making processes.

You may have noticed that this circular (rather than graduated) model of involvement does not place value on any of the different levels, in the sense that one level is seen as better or higher than another. By adopting a person-centred approach, the model recognises that different forms of involvement may be best for different service users and carers at different times, according to their circumstances. The model provides for the negotiation of appropriate levels of participation, depending on the nature of the task and the different types of decision-making processes required, so that service users and carers can participate in ways that are relevant, appropriate and meaningful to them.

Arguably, to achieve full and genuine participation, service users and carers need opportunities to be involved as equal partners at every stage of service planning, service delivery, review and development: from inception, through planning, implementation, monitoring and evaluation of services. The reality is, however, that service users and carers can only participate actively in a climate that encourages their ongoing involvement and empowerment. We know that organisations are at different stages of developing participatory practices from the various Local Authority Joint Review Reports that can be downloaded from the Audit Commission website. Different levels of participation are valid, therefore, not only for different groups of service users and carers, but also at different stages of an organisation's development.

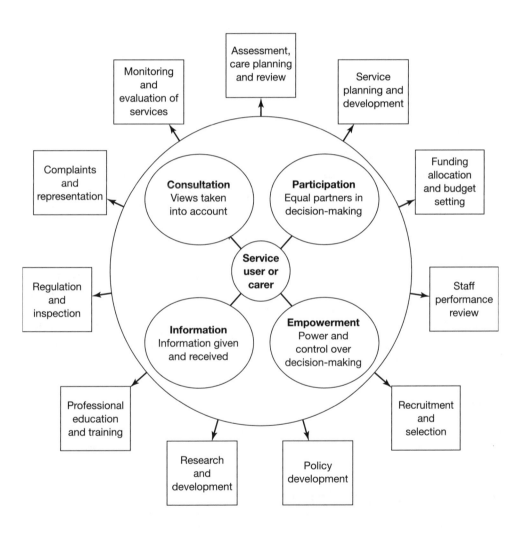

Figure 3.1 A holistic model of service user and carer involvement

Social workers need to be able to understand and distinguish the different levels of empowerment afforded to service users and carers by their own organisations, so that they are better equipped to support service user and carer participation and involvement. The following activity will enable you to think about the different levels of participation in operation within an organisation known to you.

ACTIVITY **3.2**

Think of a social work or social care organisation that you are familiar with. In what ways does the organisation engage with service users and carers?

Think about the different activities of the organisation; for example, individual case management; team planning; service development and review; research. Identify the different levels of service user and carer involvement for each activity, providing examples of how service users or carers are involved; for example, are they informed, asked to approve, invited to help make decisions?

Then think about what information or support service users and carers might need to participate more fully.

(Adapted from TEAMWISE Using research evidence: A practical guide for teams. Research in Practice, 2005)

Comment

Whilst this exercise can be helpful in clarifying the different levels at which an organisation operates in supporting service user and carer involvement, some caution is needed. It is important to bear in mind that it may not always be feasible or appropriate for an organisation to aspire to achieve full participation. Different levels of participatory practice may be appropriate to different situations according to the circumstances, goals, type of organisation, and the service users or carers involved. Individual case variables, for example, are likely to impact on, and influence, both the nature and extent of service users' and carers' participation or involvement. In some situations, partnership may be possible at a given point, but may then subsequently cease to be a reality because of changes in circumstances or shifting levels of trust between individuals and professionals. For participation to be effective, therefore, both the level of activity and the level of involvement need to be negotiated with service users and carers, so that they feel comfortable with the process and have a sense of ownership of it. Every individual should be included as much as he or she wants to be:

> *What is important is that the choice is there, and that the involvement – or partnership – is real.*

> (Janzon and Law, 2003, p3)

Barriers to participation

Effective service user and carer involvement requires genuine commitment on the part of service providers and policy-makers. In the preceding chapters, we have explored some of the incentives for engaging service users and carers, and have also identified some of the areas where service users and carers have made a real impact on outcomes. So why then has progress been patchy? What are the barriers or obstacles that prevent individuals and groups of service users and carers from participating in the decision-making processes that affect their lives?

Identify the barriers to full and genuine service user and carer participation at:

(a) the individual level (e.g. individual decision-making in assessment; construction of care and support packages);

(b) the organisational level (e.g. strategic planning; service review and development; research).

Comment

Research, inspection reports and narrative accounts from service users and carers suggest that participation in change, at both the individual and organisation level, remains restricted by a range of obstacles as shown in the box below. As can be seen, the principal barriers identified in the literature relate to power differentials and dynamics between service users, carers and professionals:

> *... power sharing can be difficult within established mainstream structures, formal consultation mechanisms and traditional ideologies.*

(Carr, 2004, pvii)

Barriers to participation and change

The individual level

Professional attitudes and assumptions:
- *assume control and power* (Crawford, Rutter and Thelwall, 2003) – *consultation rather than involvement* (Janzon and Law, 2003);

- *'know best' attitudes* (Janzon and Law, 2003);

- *fixed attitudes that are stereotypical, prejudiced and discriminatory* (Sainsbury Centre for Mental Health, 2002; Chahal and Ullah, 2004);

- *marginalisation of service users on the basis of their age, race or disability* (Thornton, 2000; Danso et al., 2003; Begum, 2006); *'hidden' nature of caring* (Becker et al., 1998; Roulstone et al., 2006).

Poor communication with service users and carers:
- *lack of information about the reasons for social work involvement* (Danso et al., 2003); *the nature and specific effects of an illness or condition* (Roulstone et al., 2006); *rights and entitlements* (Danso et al., 2003); *services available* (Chahal and Ullah, 2004); *reasons for decisions made* (Danso et al., 2003); *options available* (Swindon People First, 2000, cited in Williams, 2003, p9);

- *over-reliance on formal processes e.g. reviews* (Danso et al., 2003);

- *complaints procedures not publicised adequately* (Crawford, 2003).

Service user and carer perceptions and experiences:

- *self-rationing by carers who do not expect that services or resources will be available* (Arksey, 2002, cited in Roulstone et al., 2006, p23); *service users' perceptions of limited resources restrict choices made at assessment* (Hardy et al., 1999, cited in Janzon and Law, 2003, p11);

- *professionals lack sensitivity to the impact of stigma and social exclusion* (SCMH, 2002);

- *assume that they will not be listened to* (Danso et al., 2003); *views not taken into account* (Roulstone et al., 2006);

- *fears that comments, complaints or criticism about services could risk retaliation and withdrawal of support* (Simons, 1995; Crawford et al., 2003; Begum, 2006);

- *black and minority ethnic people's mistrust and fear of services* (SCMH, 2002; Begum, 2006);

- *feel powerless to influence own day-to-day services* (Janzon and Law, 2003);

- *professionals lack understanding of cultural traditions and the impact of racism on people's lives* (SCMH, 2002; Roulstone et al., 2006);

- *professionals focus on person with care needs at the expense of carers* (Arksey, Jackson, Wallace, Baldwin, Golder, Newbronner and Hare, 2003).

Institutional structures and practices:

- *systems complex and confusing* (Hardy et al., 1999, cited in Janzon and Law, 2003, p11);

- *strict eligibility and assessment criteria for access to support services imposed* (Barnes, Mercer with Din, 2003);

- *cash ceilings imposed on direct payments – service users risk support being withdrawn* (Barnes et al., 2003);

- *ineffective complaints procedures* (SCMH, 2002; Crawford et al., 2003) *and review systems* (Janzon and Law, 2003; Roulstone et al., 2006);

- *limited care management capacity:*

  - *high staff turnover* (Danso et al., 2003); *staff shortages* (SCMH, 2002);

  - *lack of continuity, competence and commitment of staff* (Janzon and Law, 2003);

  - *difficulties getting hold of staff* (Roulstone et al., 2006).

Lack of time:

- *delays in making or implementing decisions* (Danso et al., 2003);

- *to prepare for meetings, conferences, court hearings* (Danso et al., 2003).

The organisational level

Professional and organisational resistance:

- *organisational culture resistant to participation* (Rose et al., 2003);

- *gaps between policy, practice and knowledge* (Ramcharan and Grant, 2001, cited in Williams, 2003, p4);

- *lack of commitment to act on service users' views* (Janzon and Law, 2003);

- *lack of organisational capacity to respond to service users' change agenda* (Janzon and Law, 2003).

Professional attitudes and assumptions:

- *power differentials between professionals, service users and carers* (Rose et al., 2003; Audit Commission/SSI, 2004);

- *participation seen as the responsibility of another person or agency* (Danso et al., 2003);

- *participation seen as a fruitless exercise* (Danso et al., 2003);

- *assumptions about expert knowledge* (Crawford et al., 2003); *lack of recognition of service user competence* (Rose et al., 2003);

- *articulate service users not seen as representative* (Rose et al., 2003);

- *participation not a priority or as relevant to black and minority ethnic service users* (Begum, 2006) *leads to providers stereotyping service users and carers as wanting to take care of their own* (Begum, 2006; Roulstone et al., 2006).

Poor communication with service users and carers:

- *lack of information for service users and carers to make informed decisions* (Danso et al., 2003);

- *lack of honest information creating confusion and disillusionment* (Janzon and Law, 2003);

- *lack of feedback about how views have been used* (Audit Commission/SSI 2002, 2003; Danso et al., 2003) *leading to consultation or involvement fatigue* (Barnes et al., 2003; Begum, 2006);

- *unreasonable professional expectations that service users speak the 'managerial language'* (Crawford et al., 2003);

- *traditional participation methods, e.g. meetings and committees, not always relevant or appropriate to service users* (Begum, 2006).

Service user and carer perceptions and experiences:

- *lack of specific forums to meet for support or express views, e.g. parents of children with disabilities* (Audit Commission/SSI, 2003);

- *views not taken seriously by professionals* (Audit Commission/SSI, 2003); *expectations that nothing will change* (Danso et al., 2003);

- *forums involve too much 'talking' and 'jargon' with insufficient impact on services* (Audit Commission/SSI, 2004);

- *representation too closely regulated by managers* (Fletcher, 1995 and Ross, 1995, both cited in Barnes et al., 2003, p21);

- *feel over-researched; want action that will bring about change and to be involved in decisions that affect their lives at local and national levels* (Butt and O'Neil, 2004);

- *carers not identifying themselves as carers* (Arksey et al., 2003);

- *lack of recognition of caring role and awareness of carer's issues and needs* (Arksey et al., 2003);

- *inadequate support to discharge responsibilities on joint planning forums* (Audit Commission/SSI, 2004);

- *direction of central and local policy working against what service users want, e.g. service users' value assistance to promote independence but mainstream services targeting people with high dependency needs* (Janzon and Law, 2003).

Institutional structures and practices:
- *too formal, complex and bureaucratic* (Crawford et al., 2003; Danso et al., 2003);

- *problems associated with service users and carers being grafted onto existing planning and operational structures* (Crawford et al., 2003);

- *lack of organisational expertise in engaging with service users and carers* (Crawford et al., 2003);

- *consultation with black and minority ethnic professionals and community leaders, rather than direct discussion with service users* (Begum, 2006);

- *regional variations in carers involvement and influence in services* (Roulstone et al., 2006);

- *lack of resources* (Rose et al., 2003; Roulstone et al., 2006).

Lack of time:

- *professionals underestimate time required to set up projects and listen to service users' views; deadlines unrealistic for completing tasks* (Danso et al., 2003).

Obstacles similar to those outlined above pose challenges to all social care organisations. So what can social workers do to overcome such barriers? How can we make service user and carer participation a reality?

Facilitating participatory practice

If service users and carers are to participate more fully in affecting and shaping policy and service development, then their involvement must be real and genuine, rather than tokenistic. As we have seen, one of the biggest barriers to the achievement of participation is professionals' inability to distinguish between 'partnership', 'consultation' and 'information sharing'. This is reflected, most visibly, in service user and carer participation initiatives that:

> *... can become consultation exercises to approve of service planning and policy proposals, rather than enabling service users to be key players or partners in their formulation.*

> (Carr, 2004, p17)

In consequence, service users and carers have themselves grown used to receiving invitations to participation exercises that are tokenistic, where their participation is 'managed' by professionals (Braye, 2000).

Ultimately, effective partnership can be achieved only through equality between partners. Social work and social care professionals, therefore, have an important role to play in facilitating participation that engages service users and carers as partners in decision-making processes, for:

> *Embedded, continuous but varied participation approaches which engage service users as partners in decision making seem to have most potential for influencing change.*

> (Carr, 2004, pvii)

Let us think then for a moment about what this means in practice, as we consider some of the key requirements for effective participatory practice.

ACTIVITY 3.4

Imagine that your social work team is planning a new community initiative. How can you ensure that you include service users or carers in the development of this initiative in a way that is meaningful?

Comment

Social work and social care professionals have an important role to play in facilitating and supporting service user and carer participation. When you started to think about the above activity, one of your first thoughts may have been the need for your team to develop a strategy identifying clear aims and objectives for participation. To ensure that participation is meaningful and not tokenistic, it would be particularly important for service users and carers to be involved at the very beginning of the initiative. You would need to think carefully about who, and how many, service users and/or carers to involve in the planning and implementation of the initiative, ensuring a balance of people with regard to representation of gender, sexual orientation, race, age and disability. It would be important to include more than just one or two 'token' service users or carers, and to also ensure the inclusion of diverse and marginalised perspectives such as those of black and minority ethnic communities, children and young people with disabilities, or people with HIV/AIDS. You would need to be mindful that some professionals in your team might question the involvement of some service users or carers on the basis of assumptions about their competency or decision-making capacities. If this happened, you would need to be prepared to challenge these views so that they did not get in the way of the team's efforts to be more inclusive. Consideration would also need to be given to providing appropriate levels of support to enable service users and carers to participate. This would need to include providing an accessible venue, suitable transport, relief care, advocacy services including the use of interpreters or signers, and preparation and training to ensure that unnecessary barriers were not created. It would also be important to provide service users and carers with clear information about the level and nature of involvement on offer, levels of pay and reimbursement of expenses, and channels of complaint should they become dissatisfied with any aspect of the participation process. Moreover, it would be important to be open and honest with service users and carers about the constraints on time and resources that might obstruct progress, and to work with them to develop a plan of action that could address these issues. Listening to service users and carers, and being willing to learn from their knowledge and experience, would be crucial to the success of your initiative. As a team you would need to ensure that there was an open agenda, and that you were accepting of and receptive to the use of non-traditional participation methods and creative approaches, so that you could act upon service user and carer ideas that might challenge existing ways of working. This would help service users and carers to feel that their expertise was valued and that they had a real say in decisions about the initiative. Meeting regularly with service users and carers and giving regular updates on progress would also be important in letting them know how their views were being acted upon.

Learning organisations and the development of a culture of participation

The development of effective and meaningful participation demands that organisations make changes, so that their staff are able to listen more openly to service users and carers, and respond more effectively to their needs. In the past, participation has tended to be a one-off activity, rather than being embedded within agencies (Kirby, Lanyon, Cronin and Sinclair, 2003a). In order to increase participation and involvement and make it more integral to social work organisations, changes need to be made that help to develop infrastructures and cultures that are more participatory. This demands that staff work in different ways, which requires:

> ... *more than just sending individuals on training courses. It is about managing a process of change across an organisation, which may well face resistance, personal and organisational.*

> (Kirby et al., 2003a, p57)

Wright, Turner, Clay and Mills (2006) suggest that effective participation requires that organisations adopt a 'whole systems' approach to effect change or improvement in their services. This model focuses on the development of four interacting elements:

- **a culture of participation** – shared by staff, service users and carers;

- **a structure to support participation** – effected through a participation strategy, partnership working, identification of participation champions and provision of adequate resourcing;

- **effective practice for participation** – facilitated through the creation of a suitable, safe environment, use of creative approaches, and provision of opportunities for practitioners, service users and carers to develop the knowledge, skills and experience needed;

- **effective systems to review participation** – created through the establishment of systems to monitor, evaluate and evidence processes and outcomes.

Such an approach requires that organisations become person-centred, learning organisations that are willing to experiment, reflect on practice (Kirby et al., 2003a) and make sustainable changes to existing attitudes, patterns of behaviours, established norms and values, and the traditional processes and practices upon which the social work community has traditionally organised itself. Whilst such changes are primarily driven by policy-makers, strategic and operational managers, researchers and trainers, as social workers we have a role to play in helping to change our organisations. Developing a culture of participation within an organisation is a complex but dynamic and creative process:

> *that involves eliciting and fostering enthusiasm, sharing ideas and learning through doing.*

(Kirby et al., 2003b, p24)

Listening actively to service users and carers is important in influencing and enabling such change to happen, and taking account of what they tell us is ultimately what makes their involvement meaningful. Therefore, working *with* service users and carers, sharing ideas, being willing to test out new concepts and approaches, and being willing to learn from, and with them, are just some of the important ways in which as a social worker, you will be able to help the organisation that you work for to transform itself, and to make genuine service user and carer participation a reality.

C H A P T E R   S U M M A R Y

This chapter has explored different approaches and models to the participation and involvement of service users and carers in social work practice. We have considered the importance of understanding and distinguishing between different levels of participation and power afforded to service users and carers within organisations, and explored a range of barriers that exist in practice to greater involvement and participation. We have seen that if participation is to become more integral to social work organisations, changes are required to develop infrastructures and cultures that are more participatory. Moreover, for service users and carers to participate more fully in affecting and shaping policy and service development, their involvement has to be real and genuine, rather than tokenistic. Each of us has an important role to play in facilitating such participation, and in helping to embed participation in the fabric of our own organisations. You may find this challenging, but it is important to remember that the approach that you take and the value base that you hold are important in seeking to bring about positive change.

FURTHER READING

Kirby, P, Lanyon, C, Cronin, K and Sinclair, R (2003) *Building a culture of participation. Involving children and young people in policy, service planning, delivery and evaluation. Research report.* London: Department for Education and Skills. This report can be downloaded from **www.dfes.gov.uk**

This research report offers useful ideas about how to actively involve children and young people in decision-making and encourages organisations to explore how they can develop a more participatory culture.

Chapter 4
Empowering service user and carer participation

A C H I E V I N G   A   S O C I A L   W O R K   D E G R E E

This chapter will help you to meet the following National Occupational Standards:

Key Role 1: Prepare for, and work with individuals, families, carers, groups and communities to assess their needs and circumstances.

- Work with individuals, families, carers, groups and communities to help them make informed decisions.
- Assess needs and options to recommend a course of action.

Key Role 2: Plan, carry out, review and evaluate social work practice, with individuals, families, carers, groups, communities and other professionals.

- Interact with individuals, families, carers, groups and communities to achieve change and development and to improve life opportunities.
- Prepare, produce, implement and evaluate plans with individuals, families, carers, groups, communities and professional colleagues.

Key Role 3: Support individuals to represent their needs, views and circumstances.

- Advocate with, and on behalf of, individuals, families, carers, groups and communities.
- Prepare for, and participate in decision-making forums.

Key Role 6: Demonstrate professional competence in social work practice.

- Work within agreed standards of social work practice and ensure own professional development.

It will also introduce you to the following academic standards as set out in the social work subject benchmark statements:

1.12 Nature and extent of the subject

- Engage with service users in ways that are characterised by openness, reciprocity, mutual accountability and explicit recognition of the powers of the social worker and the legal context of intervention.

2.4 Defining principles

- Understand the impact of injustice, social inequalities and oppressive social relations.
- Help people to gain, regain or maintain control of their own affairs, insofar as this is compatible with their own or others' safety, well-being and rights.

3.1.1 Social work services and service users

- The nature of social work services in a diverse society.

3.1.2 The service delivery context

- The significance of legislative and legal frameworks and service delivery standards.

3.1.3 Values and ethics

- The nature, historical evolution and application of social work values.
- The moral concepts of rights, responsibility, freedom, authority and power inherent in the practice of social workers as moral and statutory agents.
- The complex relationships between justice, care and control in social welfare and the practical and ethical implications of these.

3.1.5 The nature of social work practice
- The nature and characteristics of skills associated with effective practice, both direct and indirect, with a range of service users and in a variety of settings.

The subject skills highlighted to demonstrate this knowledge in practice include:
3.2.2 Problem-solving skills
3.2.2.1 Managing problem-solving activities.
3.2.2.2 Gathering information.
3.2.2.3 Analysis and synthesis.
3.2.2.4 Intervention and evaluation.
3.2.3 Communication skills
- Listen actively to others, engage appropriately with the life experiences of service users, understand accurately their viewpoint and overcome personal prejudices to respond appropriately to a range of complex personal and interpersonal situations.
3.2.4 Skills in working with others
- Involve users of social work services in ways that increase their resources, capacity and power to influence factors affecting their lives.
- Consult actively with others, including service users, who hold relevant information or expertise.
- Act co-operatively with others, liaising and negotiating across differences such as organisational and professional boundaries and differences of identity or language.
- Develop effective helping relationships and partnerships with other individuals, groups and organisations that facilitate change.
5.1.2 Subject skills and other skills
- A developed capacity to integrate clear understanding of ethical issues and codes of values and practice with their interventions in specific situations.

Introduction

Empowerment is a contested concept (Adams, 2003) which is defined differently depending on people's assumptions and ideological perspectives (Starkey, 2003). Each one of us holds different experiences of being empowered, which will have informed our understanding of what empowerment means for us (Dalrymple and Burke, 1999). These experiences may have involved gaining more choice and control over our own lives and circumstances; putting our own point of view forward and being listened to; becoming aware of, and using our personal strengths; or perhaps engaging in collective action to challenge discrimination and oppression in our lives. In each of these examples, you will have noticed that there is a focus on the positive connotations of power: gaining control and reducing dependency; gaining autonomy and maximising potential.

Genuine empowerment, within the context of service user and carer participation, calls for a shift in the balance of power. As we saw in Chapter 2, social work has historically centred on the imbalance of power between professionals, service users and carers. Social workers can exercise considerable power and control by virtue of their professional training, their role as representatives of agencies with statutory powers and duties and their command of resources (Community Care Needs Assessment Project, 2001). Moves to involve service users and carers in planning their own care packages or in planning changes to service delivery, strategy or policy may, therefore, require a radical shift in perspective. At the very least, it requires a commitment to a set of values and ethical principles that treats people as equals and promotes the social inclusion of all:

> *empowerment is not an intervention or a strategy. Rather it is a fundamental way of thinking.*

(McDougall, 1997, p4)

The approach and value base of individual practitioners are crucial, therefore, in seeking to promote service user and carer participation.

In this chapter, we shall provide opportunities for you to reflect on your own thoughts and feelings about service user and carer participation. Feelings are a fundamental part of social work practice, and our awareness of, and sensitivity to, both our own and other people's feelings, is crucial to good participatory practice. Feelings can, as Thompson suggests, influence our practice, sometimes without us being aware of it, and *can colour our perceptions and shape our actions* (Thompson, 1996, p128). It is important, therefore, that we reflect on our personal feelings and attitudes about sharing power, and about increasing service user and carer control over their lives and circumstances. Service users and carers have much to teach us, but the nature and extent of our learning will be dependent, in part, upon how receptive we are to these new learning opportunities. In this chapter, we will, therefore, also explore service user and carer perceptions of social workers, examining some of the desirable qualities and attributes that they have said that they would like to see in a social worker.

Although the approach and value base of individual practitioners are an important feature of empowering practice, the effective participation of service users and carers is also dependent upon strong organisational commitment to the values and principles of involvement. In the second part of the chapter, we will examine the values and principles underpinning social work practice, and will begin to consider how these values and principles can be put into action to make service user and carer involvement for organisations and services a reality.

Personal feelings and professional practice

As we saw in Chapter 3, one of the biggest barriers to service user and carer participation is professional attitudes. As a social worker, it is important that you are able to get in touch with how you think and feel about involving service users and carers, so that you can evaluate the constraints that your perceptions may place on your relationships with them, and their subsequent engagement in participation activities. Our aim in this section of the chapter, therefore, is to encourage you to reflect on the images that you carry around with you about service user and carer participation in social work practice, and to question the attitudes, values and knowledge that inform your particular viewpoint.

ACTIVITY *4.1*

The statements below reflect some of the popular beliefs that are held about service user and carer participation. Read each of the statements in turn and record your initial responses to each. Think about how much you agree or disagree with the statements and the reasons for your response. You may like to share your views with a partner or colleague.

Statements:

1. *It's important that in empathising with service users and carers, social workers don't get too close or reveal anything about their own experiences.*

2. *Children don't know what's best for them. They have limited knowledge, skills or experience to make decisions about service or policy development.*

3. *People with learning difficulties are not capable of forming opinions and are easily influenced by others.*

4. *There's no point service user or carer reps attending committee meetings when they never say anything. The council is just ticking boxes.*

5. *Social workers are highly qualified, skilled professionals – experts in their field. You wouldn't expect a car mechanic to ask customers to diagnose what's wrong with their vehicle.*

6. *Involving people with learning difficulties in service planning or development meetings really isn't cost effective.*

7. *Service users can be ill, forgetful or even dangerous. You should only invite those people who you know are going to be reliable.*

8. *We shouldn't be listening to one or two service users or carers; after all their views are not representative.*

9. *Social workers need to protect service users and carers from having to make decisions that might cause them pain or lead to feelings of guilt.*

10. *Social work training programmes shouldn't involve service users or carers in the assessment of students' learning because this breaches confidentiality.*

11. *Carers need support; they haven't got the time to take on additional responsibilities.*

12. *Older people are not interested in shaping local services – they just want to live a relaxing, stress-free life and enjoy their well-earned retirement.*

13. *Service user and carer expectations are too high and often unrealistic.*

14. *You have to have real expertise and skill to involve service users who've experienced a head injury, stroke or have dementia.*

Comment

This activity has provided you with an opportunity to reflect on the foundations of your own judgements about service user and carer participation. You may have agreed, or partly agreed, with some of the statements, and perhaps, disagreed with others. Whatever your own personal response, it is worth noting that the statements above are typical of the many excuses that are used in practice for not involving service users or carers.

Promoting the participation of service users and carers requires genuine commitment and a willingness on the part of professionals to recognise service users and carers as experts about their own lives. Sadly, decisions about people's treatment, care or the services and support that they receive are sometimes made *about* rather than *with* them. Such paternalism exists in all social and health care services but can be compounded further by a belief that service users and carers are incapable of taking part in the decision-making processes that affect their lives. Many social work constructions of childhood, for example, understand childhood as a state of becoming rather than one of being, and present the experience of children in terms of their incapacity and naivete rather than in terms of their strengths and experiences (Butler and Roberts, 1997). Similarly, as highlighted in Activity 4.1, the views of mental health service users may be discounted as being unrealistic or a function of their mental health problems, whilst those of people with learning difficulties may be dismissed on account of their tendency to acquiesce or to experience problems transferring learning between different situations (Finlay and Lyons, 2002 and Cashdan, 1973, both cited in Williams, 2003, p1). Such perceptions, however, act directly to exclude service users and carers from involvement in decision-making processes. Being more aware of the presumptions that you bring to your own work, therefore, is important in thinking about how you can meet each individual service user and carer on his or her own terms, without imposing your own meanings on the nature or level of their participation.

The creation of environments and contexts in which service users and carers can gain power and control over decision-making in their lives is crucial, if genuine service user and carer participation is to become a reality. The ways in which service users' and carers' views are obtained in care planning, service delivery, strategy or policy development is important in this respect. Clare and Cox (2003), for example, observe that in individual programme planning (IPP) for people with learning difficulties, the degree of genuine participation varies considerably. This view is supported by research findings such as those outlined in the summary below.

RESEARCH SUMMARY

An evaluation of an established individual programme planning service for people with learning difficulties found that people who needed others to speak on their behalf were excluded from discussion during their meetings more frequently than they were included. Moreover, whilst service users who were able to speak for themselves were included in their meeting more than they were excluded, they appeared to have no influence on the format of the meeting or on its process. Recommendations reinforced the importance of individualising the planning process, by adopting communication methods appropriate to each individual and using the support of speech and language therapists at the develop-mental stages. The study also highlighted the need for a more person-centred approach, giving service users more control over the format of the meeting and its content.

(Carnaby, 1997)

Such research highlights the gap that exists in practice between the rhetoric of inclusion and the reality of experience for some groups of service users, particularly those with complex needs such as people with significant cognitive impairments, or those with whom service planners and providers find it hard to communicate (Clare and Cox, 2003).

Unless well thought out, there can be a real threat of tokenism, moreover, when service user and carer involvement appears to be motivated primarily by a need to appear to be complying with policy directives (Clare and Cox, 2003) or as is commonly referred to as the 'ticking boxes' approach. You may have attended meetings, committees or forums, for example, that function as reporting sites for developments and decisions made elsewhere. People often find it hard to contribute to these kinds of meetings, particularly when they are built around formal agendas and procedures that are dominated by health and care professionals. Such processes can give rise to a number of problems which can lead to service users and carers feeling disempowered, excluded and marginalised. Their voices may be ignored, for example, because they are felt to be unrepresentative of a particular group of service users based on their experience of involvement, their views, or personal characteristics (such as age, class and education) (Beresford and Campbell, 1994). Also the use of professional jargon may exclude some service users and carers, making it difficult for their voices to be heard. Therefore, whilst the requirement for participation may in theory be met, the reality is that professionals can continue to maintain power and control over such processes. A genuine concern to hear the voices of service users and carers and to involve them fully in shaping services demands a willingness on the part of professionals to shift the balance of power further towards service users and carers.

In reflecting on Activity 4.1, we must conclude that whilst the involvement of service users and carers in formal meetings is important, it is equally important to make sure that people are being invited because their contribution is needed and valued:

The key challenge for professionals is one of creating accepting contexts that allow inclusion to become a reality.

(Clare and Cox, 2003, p126)

Establishing environments that enable service users and carers to feel accepted for who they are and what they bring is important, therefore, if their inclusion in participatory activities is to be genuine. In practice, this may mean meeting with service users and carers prior to meetings to exchange information, clarify queries, accept proposals or agenda items, and to make arrangements for any support that may be needed during or following meetings. It may also mean providing training to enable staff to consider how they can work with service users and carers to create structures and environments that are more inclusive.

Service user and carer perceptions of social workers

Effective participation in social work practice is dependent on sensitive and effective practitioners who are able to listen to service users and carers, and deliver the kinds of services that people need and want. Many service users and carers know exactly what it is that they want social workers to be like based on their previous experience of professional involvement generally, and their present hopes and expectations. The next activity will enable you to think about what you would want from a social worker.

ACTIVITY 4.2

Imagine that you are one of the following:

- *a looked-after child or young person;*

- *an adult who uses services for older people, people with a mental illness or learning difficulty;*

- *a young or adult carer.*

If you have personal experience as a service user or carer, you may wish to choose an alternative perspective from the list above for the purposes of this activity.

Design a poster or collage portraying your ideal social worker. Identify the personal qualities and characteristics that you would hope to see in that person.

Comment

When thinking about the above activity, you perhaps started by identifying individuals who have made a difference to your own life, and considered the qualities in them that made their relationship with you special. The quality of the relationships that social workers have with service users and carers is equally important: through these relationships, you too have the potential to make a positive difference to other people's lives. The personal qualities listed in the summaries below are what service users and carers tell us they would like to see in a social worker.

ACTIVITY 4.3

Read through the summaries below, and think about how the research presented can inform your own future practice. You may like to keep a record of your thoughts so that you can return to this activity in the future to remind yourself about what matters to service users and carers.

What do adult service users and their carers want their social workers to be like?

In developing the new social work degree, the Department of Health set up a series of focus groups which involved key stakeholders not traditionally seen as having a voice in social work education and training, namely service users, carers, students, frontline social workers and employment agencies. These groups were briefed with identifying changes that were required in social work education and training to improve the delivery of services to services users (Barnes, 2002). Their report summarised what matters to service users:

- *the need for social workers to understand what a person's life is really like, and not to make assumptions and judgements about what they think the person wants or needs;*

- *the importance of the quality of the relationships that the social worker has with the service user (Barnes, 2002).*

It also highlighted the personal qualities that service users would like to see in a social worker:

- *physically and emotionally available;*

- *supportive, encouraging and reassuring;*

- *respectful;*

- *patient and attentive to the service users' problems;*

- *committed to the independence of the individual;*

- *punctual;*

- *trustworthy;*

- *reliable;*

- *friendly but not frightened to tell people how they see things;*

- *empathic and warm.*

Similarly, what carers wanted of social workers was:

- *'someone who will listen to me AND understand what I am saying';*

- *'someone who knows and can evaluate my situation';*

- *'someone who is there "for me"';*

- *'someone who prevents crises';*

- *'someone capable of thinking laterally';*

- *'"I can't do it but I know someone who can"attitude';*

- *'someone who is objective and non-judgemental'.*

Source: Reform of social work education and training. Focus on the future. Key messages from focus groups about the future of social work training (Barnes, 2002).

What do children and young people want their social workers to be like?

One of the main roles of the Children's Rights Director for England is to find out young people's views about the social care services that they receive from their local councils. The Children's Views Report 'About Social Workers' (Morgan, 2006) produced by the team in the Office of the Children's Rights Director outlines what children and young people, who receive help from children's social care services, or who are living away from home in children's homes, residential special schools or in foster care, say about social workers. Children and young people want people to be recruited as social workers who:

- *are outgoing, not stuck-up and get on with children and young people;*
- *keep promises;*
- *are in tune with young people;*
- *are approachable, easy to talk to;*
- *can listen and be bothered;*
- *have a 'thick skin';*
- *have a sense of humour;*
- *are good at calming other people down when they are upset;*
- *don't judge people but understand;*
- *are good planners and push to get things done;*
- *genuinely want to help, not just paid to help;*
- *are likely to stay in the job;*
- *are patient;*
- *are practical and down to earth;*
- *are friendly, sociable, caring and compassionate;*
- *don't nag;*
- *are reliable and punctual;*
- *help children to have a say.*

Comment

Whilst service users and carers report both positive and negative experiences of social workers, the clear message from these reports is that social workers' personal attributes can make all the difference to service users and carers. Individual qualities are, therefore, an important component of empowering social work practice.

The value-base underpinning service user and carer participation

If genuine participation and empowerment are dependent upon practitioners treating service users and carers as partners, each capable of bringing their qualities, knowledge, skills and experience to the relationship, then this, in turn, requires individual awareness and understanding of the values and operational principles underpinning participation. However, whilst the values of social work are a distinctive feature of the profession (Higham, 2005), considerable ambiguity exists about how they are defined, and the extent to which they describe what is happening in current practice, or whether in reality, they represent a set of aspirations that need to shape and mould the character of future service provision (Waine, Tunstill and Meadows, 2005). We do not intend to examine this debate here, but if you are interested in exploring these issues further, you can download a report by Waine et al. (2005) which reviews the evidence about the principles and values underpinning the provision of social care in Britain. Further details about where to obtain a copy of this report can be found at the end of this chapter.

It is generally acknowledged that the key values underpinning current social work practice include the right to choose, the right to respect, privacy and confidentiality, the promotion of independence and treating people as individuals (Levin, 2004). Traditionally, however, as we saw in Chapter 2, the social work value base has been founded on assumptions about practitioners needing to be 'experts', *who imposed their frames of understanding and their methods of intervention upon service users and carers* (Tew, Gell and Foster, 2004, p10). Arguably, one of social work's most successful achievements, therefore, has been the way in which the profession has reviewed and adapted its value base over time by drawing on new ideas from outside of social work (Higham, 2005).

Influences on social work values

As a set of beliefs, principles or assumptions, social work values have been influenced over time by a wide variety of sources. Parker (2005) in *Effective practice learning in social work* identifies seven such sources:

- individual social workers;
- cultures and communities;
- religion;
- politics;
- philosophical and academic traditions;
- social work agencies;
- society.

An eighth source, which can be added to this list, is the service user and carer movements. As we saw in Chapter 2, the service user movement has for many years stressed the value of models of participation that are based on equality, human rights, inclusion and the social model of disability (Levin, 2004). These approaches, which centre on the empowerment of individuals and the implementation of anti-oppressive and anti-discriminatory practices (Levin, 2004), have impacted on social work practice. In consequence, a different value base has been emerging within health care and social work practice based on the principles of partnership between practitioners, service users and carers (Tew *et al.*, 2004; Higham, 2005). As Levin states:

Taken together, the values of service user organisations and of social work provide a firm foundation on which to build a framework for participation that is respectful and meaningful rather than tokenistic.

(Levin, 2004, p11)

CASE STUDY

Vicky, a 48-year-old mother of two children, is a wheelchair user. She has experience of working as a nurse with people who have learning difficulties and is currently employed as an access auditor and counsellor. She writes:

My own experience of social work/social workers has been positive in the main ... I have found that within the social work field (although it is diminishing), the medical model not the social model of disability can still be found. There is still an underlying patronising attitude of 'we know best'. I am very lucky that I have a social worker who believes wholeheartedly in the social model of disability ... If I had not been a person with a little knowledge within social care, I would not even have been given a community care assessment, as when I phoned up, the person on the phone tried to brush me aside. What would have happened if I had been a vulnerable person and had been treated like this? We as disabled people must be seen as individuals not a block of people to be catered for en masse. SEE THE INDIVIDUAL NOT THE IMPAIRMENT!!!

Society also holds a set of values, which influence social work practice. These values are usually enshrined in legislation and policy, and are also subject to change over time. As we saw in Chapter 2, for example, the key legislation in respect of children and young people before the Children Act 2004, was the Children Act 1989. This piece of legislation was underpinned by a clear set of values or principles including that:

- the interests of the child should be paramount;
- the state should work in partnership with parents.

(Waine et al., 2005).

The Green Paper, *Every Child Matters* (DfES, 2003), has since introduced a new hierarchy of values which underpin the government's policy framework for reducing social exclusion (Wistow, 2005).

An individual social worker's own value base is an important component of empowering practice. Values determine who we are and how we practise: what we do, how we do it and why we do it. As individuals, each of us brings a personal set of values to our work derived from our upbringing, experiences and learning which influence our attitudes and guide our behaviour. In the context of service user and carer participation, therefore, the approach and value base of each individual practitioner are important in influencing and empowering service user and carer involvement.

As social workers, it is vital that we develop an awareness of our own set of values and beliefs, and clearly identify where these may conflict with those of the social work profession or the people whose interests we serve. The Code of Practice for Social Care Workers (GSCC, 2002) provides the most recent statement of social work values (Levin, 2004), and clearly outlines the standards of professional conduct and practice that are expected of social workers in England. A similar publication has been issued for Northern Ireland (Northern Ireland Social Care Council, 2002), Wales (Care Council for Wales, 2002) and Scotland (Scottish Social Services Council, 2005). The six standards that service users, carers and the general public can expect from social workers are to:

- *protect the rights and promote the interests of service users and carers;*
- *strive to establish and maintain the trust and confidence of service users and carers;*
- *promote the independence of service users while protecting them as far as possible from harm or danger;*
- *respect the rights of service users whilst seeking to ensure that their behaviour does not harm themselves or other people;*
- *uphold public trust and confidence in social care services;*
- *be accountable for the quality of their work and take responsibility for maintaining and improving their knowledge and skills.*

(GSCC, 2002)

Each standard is further broken down into more specific behaviours that are expected of a social worker. It is important, therefore, that as a trainee social worker, you become familiar with these standards, and reflect on their meaning for your own future practice. The next activity will help you to do this, but first you will need to download the Code of Practice in full from the GSCC website, www.gscc.org.uk/codes_copies.htm

---

ACTIVITY 4.4

Return to Activity 4.1. What personal values and beliefs underpinned your view of service user and carer participation in each of the examples given?

Now compare your own set of values and beliefs with the principles set out in the Code of Practice. Identify where your own values and beliefs match or conflict with those of the social work profession. Think about the implications of this for your own future practice.

Comment

Being aware of our own value system is important for two reasons. First, it helps us to guard against manipulation and control, so that we can more readily empower service users and carers within our everyday practice. Second, it helps us to identify where conflicts may arise between our own and others' values and beliefs so that we are better prepared to deal with them.

In this section, we have identified a number of different value systems, all of which interact with, and influence social work practice. Inevitably, tensions can arise between these different sets of value systems, *the most fundamental being those between 'caring' and 'control'* (Wistow, 2005, p11). Arguably, a potential clash of values is most likely in the fields of mental health and child protection, where the social worker's 'policing' role does not sit easily with the concept of social inclusion (Waine et al., 2005). In the field of mental health, for example, government policy emphasises the importance of promoting the social inclusion of people with a mental illness (DoH, 1999d). However, alongside this, approved social workers are expected to operate within a legal framework that provides, where necessary, for the protection of vulnerable individuals and the general public by compulsory admission to hospital.

As the 'guardians of values' (Higham, 2005), it is important that social workers keep their professional values at the forefront of practice. In the final part of this chapter, we will start to consider the process of enshrining professional values into operational principles: in other words, putting our professional values into action.

Putting values into action

As we saw in Chapter 2, over the past decade, the service users' and carers' movements have developed clear sets of principles to help put their values into action (see Levin, 2004). Statements of these core principles and values are outlined in strategy plans (e.g. Carers UK, 2005), research reports (e.g. Turner and Beresford, 2005), briefing papers and reports resulting from workshops and conferences (Beresford, 1994; Young Independent People Presenting Educational Entertainment (YIPPEE) and Citizens as Trainers (CATS) (2002), best practice guidelines (e.g. Turner and Shaping Our Lives National User Network, 2002) and journal articles (e.g. CATS, YIPPEE, Rimmer and Harwood, 2004)

RESEARCH SUMMARY

In 2004, Shaping Our Lives, an independent user-controlled organisation, was commissioned by the Department of Health to undertake a nationwide study of service user views as part of a government consultation to develop a new vision for adult social care. The study was based on the views of 112 social care service users from a diverse range of backgrounds gathered from different parts of the country. Taken together, service users' comments from the survey form a set of core principles and values for positive social care:

- *policy and practice for social care, not just personal care;*

- *effective user involvement;*

- *a participatory process of social care development;*

- *involving service users in defining quality;*

- *offering quality and choice on service users' terms;*

- *prioritising equality and valuing diversity;*

- *a rights-based approach to social care;*

- *social model-based social care;*

- *social care which supports people to be independent by ensuring them the support to live as they want to;*

- *social care which supports and enables service users to participate, contribute, have real choices and do things with others in the mainstream;*

- *developing direct payments;*

- *strategically supporting more user-led services;*

- *listening to service users;*

- *truly person-centred social care;*

- *improving access, improving support;*

- *an integrated approach to social care;*

- *revaluing social care.*

(Beresford et al., 2005, pvii)

Whilst there appears to be general agreement among service users, carers and their organisations about the principles and values of involvement, participation can only be effective where there is a commitment to the development of genuine partnerships between professional agencies, service users and carers, and to the development of formal agreements about the key principles underpinning such involvement. Recent participation guidance places value on the development of charters or standards for participation on which an organisation's practice is to be based (Wright et al., 2006). Such charters embody the shared principles and values that underpin partnership work, and provide a vision for involving service users and carers in decisions that affect their lives. An example of such a charter is provided below.

The Children Now *Participation Charter*, published in 2006, sets out a vision for giving children and young people a say in the decisions that affect them. It was drawn up in conjunction with experts and organisations in the field, including Participation Works and children and young people. The values and principles underpinning this charter acknowledge that:

- *participation is a right;*

- *children and young people are the best authorities on their own lives;*

- *participation depends on respect and honesty;*

- *participation must be accessible and inclusive;*

- *participation is a dialogue to influence change;*

- *participation is built in;*

- *participation is everyone's responsibility;*

- *participation benefits everybody.*

This charter is supported by the British Youth Council, Carnegie Young People Initiative, Children's Rights Alliance for England, Children's Commissioner for England, National Children's Bureau, National Youth Agency and Save the Children.

(Children Now, 2006. www.childrennow.co.uk/charter see also www.participationworks.org.uk)

Whilst charters set out the principles, standards and actions needed to promote the systematic involvement of service users and carers, the actual process of developing a charter is important to the building of a participative culture (Wright et al., 2006). The involvement of service users and carers in the design and review of a charter, for example, can be crucial in seeking to overcome some of the common barriers to participation. The *Young peoples' charter of participation* (Sketchley and Walker, 2001) developed by the staff and young people of the Rotherham Participation Project – a former project of The Children's Society – is a good example of this, as seen below.

RESEARCH SUMMARY

Using research involving over 400 children and young people, researchers collated participants' views to identify the common themes that were creating barriers to young people accessing services or being involved in decision-making at a local level. Young people were then involved in developing principles to enable organisations to actively promote participation.

(Sketchley and Walker, 2001, p1)

Building a culture of participation across service boundaries is dependent upon partner agencies also agreeing, adopting and embedding a charter into the working practices of their own organisations. Practice guidance concerning children's participation suggests that children and young people are more likely to feel confident about sharing their principles and charter with other young people or agencies who are trying to establish and develop participation, if they have been involved in regular reviews of their own agencies' charter (Wright and Haydon, 2002, cited in Wright et al., 2006, p19). Practice advice and training packages are now available to support service user and carer involvement in the development of such charters and standards. The *Young people's key skill development training manual* (2006), for example, produced by The Children's Society in collaboration with children, young people and the Carnegie UK Trust, provides an accredited training programme for developing the participatory skills of young people who have experienced exclusion and marginalisation in society. The manual for the training programme, which was originally designed to support young people's work in developing the *Young people's key charter of participation* (Sketchley and Walker, 2001), can be downloaded from www.childrenssociety.org.uk

For a participation charter to effect change, however, it needs to form part of the overall infrastructure for supporting service user and carer involvement. This has implications for an organisation's structures, practice and review (Wright et al., 2006). As Cutler (2003) states, standards or charters:

> *should be seen as only one part of a cycle of management and they need to be backed by resources, training, inspection and evaluation.*

> (Cutler, 2003, p5)

One of the main ways that an organisation can evidence its commitment to participation is by reflecting the values and principles laid down in its charter in all of its policies, procedures and practice frameworks, including job descriptions, strategic plans, policy guidelines and practice manuals (Wright et al., 2006). The next activity will provide an opportunity for you to consider whether there is a strong commitment to involving service users and carers at the heart of the core values of an organisation known to you.

ACTIVITY 4.5

Locate copies of local charters, statements, policies and procedures for service user and carer involvement in the area in which you are living or working. These documents can include:

- *participation charters for young people, adult service users and carers;*

- *policy and procedural documents for involving service users and carers in decision-making processes such as recruitment and selection;*

- *service user and carer strategy/action plans for involving service users and carers.*

Read through the documents and identify the values and principles underpinning organisational practice/statements.

A number of voluntary and statutory sector organisations provide access to these documents online. If you are able to obtain documentation from two organisations, you could compare and contrast their different approaches. You might like to work with a colleague to make this comparison.

Although many organisations in the voluntary and statutory sector have, in recent years, adopted specific policies or some type of written statement which outline a commitment to involving service users and carers in decision-making processes:

Organisations face particular challenges in moving from policy declarations of principled support for participation, to embedding that commitment in everyday practice.

(Cutler and Taylor, 2003, p5)

This is an issue that will be explored further in the next two chapters, when we examine some of the different approaches to involving children, and adult service users and their carers in social work practice.

Before we turn in the next chapter to a discussion of how to involve adult service users and carers in shaping social work services, consider the following activity.

ACTIVITY 4.6

You may have heard people making comments similar to those listed in Activity 4.1. Using your knowledge about the benefits of service user and carer participation in social work practice discussed in this book so far, think about how you might respond in the future to critical comments or negative statements about service user or carer participation.

Comment

This activity will help to consolidate your knowledge. We have not provided examples of how you might respond, as this activity gives you an opportunity to reflect on your understanding thus far.

CHAPTER SUMMARY

In this chapter, you have explored some of the key components of empowering practice. Increasing service user and carer involvement within non-user or carer controlled organisations is a complex, political process, which calls for a redistribution of power and the establishment of more equitable relationships between practitioners, service users and carers. In practice, this demands that organisations build cultures that promote service user and carer participation. In examining participatory practice with children and young people, Kirby et al. (2003a) suggest that reducing the power imbalance involves moving away from structures and practices that seek to control young people, to more flexible environments and practices that enable them to influence change and improve services. These observations can be applied equally well to adult health and social care.

The core values and principles underpinning the service user and carer movements and social work practice provide the cornerstone for effective service user and carer involvement and participation. Building effective cultures for participation, however, demands commitment from individual social workers and their managers. As we have seen, the attributes, approaches and value base of individual social workers are important in this respect. Equally important is agreement over shared principles for involvement, and the development of genuine partnerships between professionals, service users and carers. However, without the establishment of an effective organisational infrastructure to support participation, service user and carer involvement cannot be properly sustained (Wright et al., 2006).

Adams, R (2003) *Social work and empowerment*, 3rd edn. Basingstoke: Palgrave Macmillan.

This clear and accessible book will provide you with an overview of the different theories, models and methods associated with empowerment. It offers useful discussion of empowering work with individuals, groups, communities and organisations that can be used to enhance activities, discussion and tasks presented in this chapter.

General Social Care Council (2002) *Code of Practice for Social Care Workers*. London: General Social Care Council.

This code, which reflects the shared values of the social care sector, sets out the standards of practice and conduct expected of social workers. You can download the code at **www.gscc.org.uk/Good+practice+and+conduct/What+are+the+codes+of+practice/**

Waine, B, Tunstill, J and Meadows, P with Peel, T (2005) *Developing social care: values and principles*. London: Social Care Institute for Excellence.

This report reviews the evidence about the principles and values which underpin the provision of social care in Britain. It is one of three major studies underpinning the SCIE position paper 04 *Developing social care: the past, the present and the future* (Wistow, 2005). You can gain access to this online at **www.scie.org.uk/publications/positionpapers/pp4/index.asp**

Chapter 5

Participation in practice: involving adults

This chapter will help you to meet the following National Occupational Standards:

Key Role 1: Prepare for, and work with individuals, families, carers, groups and communities to assess their needs and circumstances.

- Work with individuals, families, carers, groups and communities to help them make informed decisions.
- Assess needs and options to recommend a course of action.

Key Role 2: Plan, carry out, review and evaluate social work practice, with individuals, families, carers, groups, communities and other professionals.

- Interact with individuals, families, carers, groups and communities to achieve change and development and to improve life opportunities.
- Prepare, produce, implement and evaluate plans with individuals, families, carers, groups, communities and professional colleagues.
- Work with groups to promote individual growth, development and independence.

Key Role 3: Support individuals to represent their needs, views and circumstances.

- Advocate with, and on behalf of, individuals, families, carers, groups and communities.
- Prepare for, and participate in decision-making forums.

Key Role 5: Manage and be accountable, with supervision and support, for your own social work practice within your organisation.

- Contribute to the management of resources and services.

Key Role 6: Demonstrate professional competence in social work practice.

- Research, analyse, evaluate, and use current knowledge of best social work practice.
- Work within agreed standards of social work practice and ensure own professional development.

It will also introduce you to the following academic standards as set out in the social work subject benchmark statements:

2.4 Defining principles

- Help people to gain, regain or maintain control of their own affairs, insofar as this is compatible with their own or others' safety, well-being and rights.

3.1.3 Values and ethics

- The nature, historical evolution and application of social work values.

3.1.4 Social work theory

- Research-based concepts and critical explanations from social work theory and other disciplines that contribute to the knowledge base of social work.
- Approaches and methods of intervention in a range of community-based settings including group-care at individual, group and community levels, including factors guiding the choice and evaluation of these.

3.1.5 The nature of social work practice

- The characteristics of practice in a range of community-based and organisational settings including group-care, within statutory, voluntary and private sectors, and the factors influencing changes in practice within these contexts.

- The nature and characteristics of skills associated with effective practice, both direct and indirect, with a range of service users and in a variety of settings including group-care.
- The place of theoretical perspectives and evidence from international research in assessment and decision-making processes in social work practice.
- The integration of theoretical perspectives and evidence from international research into the design and implementation of effective social work intervention with a wide range of service users, carers and others.
- The processes of reflection and evaluation, including familiarity with the range of approaches for evaluating welfare outcomes, and their significance for the development of practice and the practitioner.

The subject skills highlighted to demonstrate this knowledge in practice include:

3.2.2 Problem-solving skills

3.2.2.1 Managing problem-solving activities.

3.2.2.2 Gathering information.

3.2.2.3 Analysis and synthesis.

3.2.2.4 Intervention and evaluation.

3.2.3 Communication skills

- Listen actively to others, engage appropriately with the life experiences of service users, understand accurately their viewpoint and overcome personal prejudices to respond appropriately to a range of complex personal and interpersonal situations.
- Use both verbal and non-verbal cues to guide interpretation.
- Identify and use opportunities for purposeful and supportive communication with service users within their everyday living situations.
- Communicate effectively across potential barriers resulting from differences.

3.2.4 Skills in working with others

- Involve users of social work services in ways that increase their resources, capacity and power to influence factors affecting their lives.
- Consult actively with others, including service users, who hold relevant information or expertise.
- Act co-operatively with others, liaising and negotiating across differences such as organisational and professional boundaries and differences of identity or language.
- Develop effective helping relationships and partnerships with other individuals, groups and organisations that facilitate change.
- Challenge others when necessary, in ways that are most likely to produce positive outcomes.

Introduction

Poor participatory practice is one of the most commonly cited obstacles to effective service user and carer participation (Wright et al., 2006). The research evidence suggests that there still appears to be a lack of opportunity for service users to be involved in making decisions about their own lives (see, for example, Carr, 2004). As we saw in Chapter 3, professional and organisational resistance (Crawford et al., 2003), exclusionary institutional structures and practices, and professional attitudes and assumptions (Carr, 2004) can make it difficult for service users' and carers' voices to be heard. The overriding message of this book, therefore, is that for service users and carers to become more fully involved in social work practice, social workers need to be able to work in ways that enable and promote their participation. This means developing ways of working that actively seek and include service user and carer perspectives, experience, knowledge and skills. It also requires that we develop a systematic approach to analysing our own value base and reflecting critically on our own practice, as we saw in Chapter 4.

In this chapter, we shall examine some of the ways and means of facilitating service user and carer involvement. We will start by examining some of the key components required for building and sustaining effective participation, focusing in particular on the organisational infrastructure, the building and sustaining of positive relationships, and the development of effective support mechanisms. In the second part of the chapter, we will explore some of the different methods and approaches that can be used to develop participatory practices with adult service users and their carers. The specific issues surrounding the involvement of children and young people in social work practice, and some of the mechanisms that can be employed in working with these service user and carer groups, will be explored in Chapter 6.

Building and sustaining participation

Building and sustaining participation is dependent upon three main variables:

- the establishment of an organisational culture and infrastructure that supports participation;

- the development of strong, positive relationships between social workers, service users and carers;

- the provision of effective practical and emotional support mechanisms.

We will now consider each of these in turn.

Organisational infrastructure

As we have seen, establishing an organisational culture that recognises the need for change, and developing organisational systems and structures that provide the means to support change (see Wright et al., 2006), are crucial to the promotion of effective participatory practices. Once the principle of participation has been adopted within an organisation, it is essential to develop the necessary infrastructure – systems, procedures, structures and resources (Cutler and Taylor, 2003) – to actively engage service users and carers, and to support their involvement in effecting change within the organisation. In a research report which 'maps' children and young people's participation in England, Oldfield and Fowler (2004, p64) note a range of organisational systems, structures and support mechanisms that are considered necessary for the effective participation of children and young people. These include:

- *written policies or strategies;*

- *monitoring or formal evaluation;*

- *dedicated participation staff;*

- *a budget controlled by children and young people;*

- *identification of a senior responsible individual;*

- *training and support for children and young people;*

- *incentives and recognition for children and young people involved in decision-making.*

This list can be applied equally well to the involvement of adult service users and carers. Research by Robson, Begum and Locke (2003) provides further examples of some of the core organisational structures, systems and support mechanisms needed to promote effective participation, as seen below.

RESEARCH SUMMARY

An action research project undertaken by Robson et al. (2003) *aimed to support and increase user involvement in four voluntary organisations. The study distinguished between 'management-centred user involvement' (where service users participate in existing structures following agendas that have been defined by the organisation) and 'user-centred user involvement' (where service users set the agenda). They found that service users only really value 'user-centred user involvement', viewing anything less as tokenism.*

Their research also suggests that change is likely to occur in organisations that:

- *focus on service user issues and priorities;*
- *have leaders who are committed, take risks, provide vision, strong direction and opportunities for change;*
- *allocate specific human and financial resources;*
- *continuously monitor and evaluate service user participation policy and practice;*
- *promote good quality two-way communication between service users and decision-makers;*
- *maximise the presence of service users in a range of organisational activities;*
- *negotiate the external support of researchers and consultants;*
- *promote equality of opportunity for service users throughout all roles in the organisation.*

Building and sustaining positive relationships

The commitment of the individual social worker to participatory practices is also important. *Participation is a way of working* (Kirby et al., 2003a, p86) which is dependent upon *the development of positive relationships* (Kirby et al., 2003a, p86) between social workers, service users and carers. Whilst professionals' individual characteristics and attributes are important in influencing both the nature and extent of involvement, the way that social workers act, engage with and support service users and carers will undoubtedly affect whether they become involved or stay involved. The next activity will provide opportunities for you to consider the factors that are required for building and sustaining positive relationships with service users and carers.

ACTIVITY 5.1

Draw a table with two columns as shown below. Think of a personal relationship in your life, past or present and list the factors that made or make it positive.

Now, think about a social worker's relationships with service users or carers. What factors will help you as a social worker to develop positive, sustainable relationships with service users and carers?

Factors that will help to develop a positive relationship

Personal relationship	Professional relationship

Whatever the level of participation, or the methods used, genuine and meaningful participation is dependent upon the development of a supportive environment based on trust, mutual respect, equity and good communication (Kirby et al., 2003a). As Carr notes:

> The research shows the importance of allowing sufficient time and support for constructive dialogue and trust building to improve partnership working.

(Carr, 2004, p28)

In enabling and encouraging service users and carers to become and stay involved, it is important to show a genuine interest in them as people. This means that we need to move past stereotypes or labels (Kirby et al., 2003a), and suspend judgements or assumptions so that we can listen more effectively to service users' and carers' priorities and issues. Establishing a constructive dialogue in which we can listen to, and learn from, service users and carers is important, therefore, in:

- understanding their perspectives, and thinking about how we can include their varying viewpoints;

- understanding their preferred ways of involvement, and accommodating alternative ways of working and communicating;

- giving service users and carers clarity about the limits of their involvement;

- enabling service users and carers to define their own criteria/outcomes for participation;

- sharing something of ourselves including our views, experiences and knowledge, whilst maintaining professional boundaries;

- exploring with service users and carers the meaning of partnership and independence;

- sharing information;

- giving ongoing feedback to service users' and carers about how their involvement and views have affected outcomes.

(Beresford and Croft, 1993; Carter and Beresford, 2000; Kirby et al., 2003a; Carr, 2004)

Building and sustaining participation takes time, it is a process, not a one-off event:

It takes time to build up respectful and purposive relationships and to give attention to the practicalities.

(Levin, 2004, p10)

Support mechanisms

Participation can place many pressures and demands on the people involved. Access to formal and informal support is, therefore, important in developing service users' and carers' skills and confidence, should they need it.

Support has been identified as one of the levers for making service user and carer participation work (Levin, 2004). Certainly, before becoming involved service users and carers need to know that any particular needs that they have will be met. Clear information is, therefore, needed about the range of support that is available to them, how it will be provided and by whom. The next activity will help you to consider the types of support that service users and carers might need.

ACTIVITY **5.2**

Read through the scenarios below and list the range of supports that might be put in place to facilitate each individual's participation:

1. Esther is white, British, 72 years old and is partially sighted. She spends most of her time caring for her husband, Luke, who has Alzheimer's disease. She has expressed interest in becoming involved in a working group to evaluate current service provision for carers in her locality. What supports could be put in place for Esther?

2. Dan is African Caribbean, 55 years old, has Down's syndrome and has, until recently, lived with his mum who provided for his full-time care. Following his mother's admission to a nursing home, Dan has had to move in with an 85-year old maiden aunt. The arrangement is temporary, however, as Dan's aunt has stated that she cannot look after him on a long-term basis. How might Dan be supported to participate in decisions about his future?

3. Amir is 40 years old and a refugee. He lost the use of both of his legs three years ago following a massacre in his home country in which his wife and three children died. He uses a wheelchair and receives ongoing mental health support services. Amir is undecided about whether to join a working group which will aim to improve access to mental health services for refugees experiencing difficulties related to their mental health. What support might Amir require to enable him to participate?

Comment

It is important to make involvement as easy as possible for people. According to Carter and Beresford (2000), two components are essential to ensure effective and inclusive involvement, no matter what method or model of participation is adopted: these are access and support. As you will have noticed from the above activity, support can take many different forms. At a practical level, the principle of paying service user and carer groups and individuals for their time and expertise, and reimbursing travel and other expenses, is widely accepted (Levin, 2004). The government's guidance document *Reward and Recognition* (DoH, 2006b) sets out the principles of best practice for reimbursement and payment for involvement; the roles and responsibilities for service users and NHS and social care organisations, and advice on the implications of paying and reimbursing service users who are in receipt of benefits. This document can be downloaded from the Department of Health website, details of which can be found at the end of this chapter. Ensuring that the practical aspects of involvement work effectively for service users and carers is an essential part of the process of building trust and developing strong relationships (Levin, 2004). You would be right in thinking that prompt and acceptable payment and reimbursement arrangements would be important in recruiting and retaining service users and carers like Esther and Amir. It would also be important to pay for the time and expenses of any personal assistants that they may require (CCNAP, 2001).

Ensuring that a venue is accessible with regard to public transport, car parking, wheelchair access, and internal layout is also important (Voluntary Action Westminster, 2006). Any potential barriers to involvement need to be identified in advance. In terms of physical access to the venue, for example, Amir may require a door-to-door taxi service, and clear information about whether the main entrance to the building can be accessed via a ramp, and whether the doors are power-assisted. It would also be important to ensure that the layout inside the building is easily negotiable by wheelchair, and has wide corridors, a lift, and accessible toilet facilities. Esther may require a venue that is close to public transport. Information beforehand about the building such as how many steps there are, how the buttons in the lift are arranged, whether there is sufficient colour contrast inside (Voluntary Action Westminster, 2006) and whether the overhead lighting in the room is sufficient to facilitate reading (CCNAP, 2001) are important factors that would need to be taken into consideration.

It is always good practice when inviting people to participate in an event, not to make assumptions about what they may need or prefer based on any labels that might have been ascribed to them, but to ask them sensitively beforehand about any personal requirements (Voluntary Action Westminster, 2006). With regard to information for participants, it is important to try to produce supporting materials that are clear and in a user-friendly form. Esther, for example, may need text to be provided in specific font sizes or on tape in advance; Dan may benefit from pictures and symbols that can help to facilitate communication, and be used to explain information to him (Simons, 1999). Amir may prefer written information to be in his first language, written specifically for purpose and not translated (CCNAP, 2001), and may also wish to use the services of an interpreter during any meetings. Using a signer or an interpreter can be tiring, so if this were the case, it would be important to build in short breaks (Voluntary Action Westminster, 2006) for Amir during the course of the event.

Participation takes time and emotional energy. Service users may require the assistance of a personal attendant, whilst carers may need to be able to buy in replacement care to cover their time commitments. Esther, for example, is likely to need the provision of relief care so that she can leave her husband for a few hours. Research suggests that funding an individual carer's time is the most prevalent form of resource support available to carers, the main source of that funding being the Carers Grant (Roulstone et al., 2006).

Advocacy is another important form of support to service users, both individuals and groups. This involves:

> *standing up for the rights of a vulnerable person, working to protect them from harm, helping them to have a voice and arguing for resources to meet their needs.*

> (Williams, 2006, p115)

A useful summary of the many different kinds of advocacy can be found in Williams (2006), *Social work with people with learning difficulties*. For our purposes, an independent advocate may be needed to represent Dan throughout the assessment and planning processes or in the initial approach to help him to have his views listened to. Dan may be very fearful of the changes that lie ahead of him and distrustful of the people around him. Moreover, like many people with learning difficulties, he may have had very little experience of choice and very little power or control over many aspects of his life (Williams, 2006). Advocacy will be important, therefore, in supporting autonomy and choice for Dan. The advocacy role can also be particularly important where service users or carers feel unsafe or intimated by the people or situations surrounding them. Living in a culture of fear, asylum seekers or refugees like Amir, for example, may feel too afraid to express their views about services or contribute to participation initiatives which they perceive may affect their refugee status or threaten the care that they receive (see Kirby et al., 2003a).

Support may, therefore, also be needed to enhance people's personal development and provide them with the skills and confidence needed to take on a participatory role. For Esther, engaging in the working group may be the only social opportunity that she has. Like many older women, and some of those from minority ethnic groups, she may not have had many opportunities to engage in public life, and may need to develop confidence to use her skills, particularly in forums that are dominated by men (CCNAP, 2001). A buddying or mentoring scheme may help to make it easier for Esther to participate. In such a scheme, Esther would be paired up with an experienced carer who might accompany her to meetings until she feels sufficiently confident to attend on her own. Research suggests that such buddying schemes:

> *make it easier for carers to become less marginalised partners.*

> (Roulstone et al., 2006, p54)

Esther may also benefit from specific training in representation, presentation or assertiveness skills to enable her to speak up. Research suggests that training is crucial in supporting service users and carers to participate meaningfully and effectively in developing service planning and delivery, as seen below.

RESEARCH SUMMARY

Ross (1995) *set out to explore the reality behind the rhetoric of service user involvement in day care services for three particular groups of user – people with physical disabilities, people with mental health problems and people with learning difficulties. Over 200 service users were interviewed in 19 day care centres across three local authority areas in the West Midlands. A further 13 service user/carer forums were visited where more than 150 service users and carers contributed to the study. The research found that the majority of service users interviewed regarded training in areas such as confidence-building, assertiveness, committee and group work skills as being fundamental to their future ability to participate actively in service planning and delivery. Staff attitudes and commitment to the principle of service user participation, and the availability of appropriate staff support, were identified as important factors in determining the extent and level of service user involvement.*

Lindow (1999) co-ordinated an evaluation of the National User Involvement Project, a four-site development project, co-ordinated by Jenny Morris, which aimed to extend the range of service users involved in commissioning decisions. Seventy-nine service users and 14 commissioners from health and social services were interviewed over a three-year period – some were also re-interviewed one year on to assess the enduring effect of the project. Other methods of data collection in addition to individual and group interviews included observation of key events and analysis of relevant documentation. The evaluation found that many commissioners were unaware of how to facilitate user involvement and that service users needed a range of support and training in order to be more fully involved in decision-making. Identified service user training needs included 'speaking up' and assertiveness courses; disability equality training and other training led by service user-trainers to raise people's confidence; guidance on purchasers' and providers' decision-making structures, and training in committee procedures, legal issues and rights, negotiating skills and equal opportunities.

As can be seen above, training provides opportunities for service users and carers to develop their personal knowledge and skills so that they are better equipped to work alongside social workers on an equal basis. Moreover, creating safe places for people such as Amir and Esther to also explore their own identities, share experiences (Singh, 2005) and examine the effects of those experiences on their lives, can also be important in laying the foundations for participation. There need to be opportunities for service users and carers who may have unresolved feelings about services or personal experiences to talk these through, so that as Heron (1998, p169) notes, *they do not bring personal or emotional baggage into formal meetings.* A range of creative arts media can be used for this purpose, including art, drama, dance, music, film, poetry, information technology and case studies or life stories, to help resolve feelings, build self-confidence and increase awareness of rights (Singh, 2005), so that service users and carers feel better equipped to participate. Rooots, which provides training and consultancy from the perspective of African Caribbean people with learning difficulties, has experience of using such creative techniques, as highlighted in the following case study.

In 2003, People in Action – Leeds trained a group of African Caribbean people with learning difficulties to develop and deliver training to local service providers. Using a range of arts media including drumming, batik, theatre, music and poetry, the team explored their own history, culture and experiences of discrimination in order to develop awareness of their own rights as black disabled people, and confidence in their knowledge and skills to deliver training to other organisations. As a result of these experiences, Rooots secured funding to develop into a social enterprise providing training and consultancy. Among its past customers are the Leeds Family Placement Service, who as a result of Rooots training have developed a strategy to increase the number of African Caribbean carers providing short term breaks. Also, the Leeds Home Farm Trust has made improvements in its care of African Caribbean residents as a result of such training.

(Singh, 2005)

Methods and approaches to involvement

Involving service users and carers in shaping future services is a long-term, ongoing, developmental process (CCNAP, 2001). As the Community Care Needs Assessment Project (2001) observed, participation is a way of working that needs to become fully integrated into the everyday practices of all health and social care organisations. For you, this means integrating participation into every aspect of your practice as a social worker. So how do we actually *do* participation, and what methods or approaches should we be using?

As can be seen from the participation literature, there is no one method or 'best' approach to ensure the effective involvement of service users and carers (CCNAP, 2001). Kirby et al., note:

Different activities are appropriate in different situations or with differing levels of support and levels of participation.

(Kirby et al., 2003a, p103)

As we saw in Chapter 3, the appropriate level of participation can be dependent on a number of variables including the context (such as time, location and culture); the task; the type of decisions being made and participants' abilities, interests and availability (Kirby et al., 2003b). The skill of the social worker, therefore, is in offering the most appropriate methods and approaches for each situation so that the purpose is achieved.

The Department of Health's practice guidance (DoH, 2003) emphasises the importance of considering a range of approaches, and determining how the different methods or approaches *fit together to establish a pattern of ongoing involvement and dialogue* (DoH, 2003, p67). The use of a range of methods and approaches will certainly encourage the involvement of a wider range of people, particularly in public decision-making processes, and has the potential to yield richer information and more creative ideas (CCNAP, 2001). Moreover, practice guidance encourages those undertaking individual and public involvement *to be creative in designing hybrids and innovations that really suit the needs of those being involved* (DoH, 2003, p67). Although methods and approaches can often be determined by professionals, providing a range of methods and approaches from which services users and carers make a choice can make the process much more accessible and effective. Service users and carers are more likely to engage and stay engaged with processes where they have ownership of the ideas proposed, and where they are involved in ways that are inclusive and which meet their needs and preferences.

Decisions about what participation activities to use need to be made once you are clear what it is that you are aiming to achieve (Kirby et al., 2003b). As you are aware, service users and carers can be involved in both individual, private decisions about their personal lives (such as what time to get up, when to eat meals or where to live) and in collective, public decision-making processes (such as which staff to appoint, how to allocate research funding or what changes need to be made to an existing service). As these decisions vary with regard to their complexity and sensitivity (Kirby et al., 2003b), consideration needs to be given to a variety of methods or approaches to ensure that the chosen approach is appropriate for the purpose.

Approaches for individual decision-making

Most activities that a social worker may use to engage individuals in personal decision-making are informal and are used on an ongoing, everyday basis. These include spending time with people learning about their lives through direct observation, talking or communicating using specific tools or systems, and participating alongside people in activities that they enjoy doing. Such informal methods can help to increase our understanding of people's individual needs when planning care, as well as informing and developing existing and new services (Kirby et al., 2003a). These approaches are important for all service users and carers, but particularly where people have complex needs and communication impairments that may make the use of more formal mechanisms of participation less accessible. Talking Mats™, for example, is an innovative method used to enable people with learning difficulties and older people with communication difficulties arising from a stroke, dementia or hearing loss, to make choices or express their views about services in a meaningful and tangible way (Cameron and Murphy, 2002; Murphy, Tester, Hubbard, Downs and MacDonald, 2005). This powerful, pictorial communication tool can be used to get to know service users; plan their daily activities; develop and maintain relationships with them; understand challenging behaviour; and explore differences of opinion (Murphy, 2003, cited in Murphy et al., 2005, p106). Similarly, dementia care mapping is an observational tool used to assess the quality of care from the perspective of a person with dementia. Research suggests that this person-centred approach aids care planning, improves individual well-being and empowers people who have dementia by increasing their choice and autonomy in day-to-day decision-making (Martin and Younger, 2000).

CASE STUDY

Jim is 80 years old and lives in a nursing home. He has dementia, which affects his ability to recall recent events and to communicate verbally. For many years prior to Jim's illness, he sang bass in his local church choir and ran an annual 'Bring and Sing' event to raise money for local charities. A new member of staff with a musical background learns of Jim's interest and approaches him to ask if he would be interested in singing whilst she accompanies him on the piano. Jim agrees and is gradually eased back into using his voice again (see

---

CASE STUDY *continued*

Killick and Allan, 2002), *initially through simple humming and then through actual singing of hymns which he can recall well. Jim appears to greatly enjoy this new recreational pursuit and is encouraged to talk in the time immediately following his singing activities. This helps in building Jim's confidence about using his voice to communicate.*

Staff are surprised at just how much Jim expresses during these one-to-one sessions. By creating an atmosphere where the use of language and appreciation of its qualities are fostered and celebrated, the carer helps to boost Jim's self-esteem, giving him a clear message that his voice, his words and his ideas are valued, and considered interesting and important (Killick and Allan, 2002, p89).

It can often be difficult in busy health and social care settings for staff to find opportunities to undertake consultation work, and to follow through on plans (Allan, 2001). *The quality of the relationship between Jim and his carer is important in this respect, as she is able to use the opportunities, which present themselves spontaneously during and following Jim's singing activities, to talk with him about aspects of the service. This helps in giving Jim greater control over his life and his care.*

People can communicate their views about the services and care that they receive through a variety of ways: through non-verbal behaviour; visual, written and other creative media, as well as by saying what they think (Kirby et al., 2003a). It is important, therefore, that as practitioners, we seek to find appropriate ways of interacting with service users, particularly where there may be cognitive or communication impairments, so that they feel able to express their views, preferences and feelings. Different methods and approaches help to provide channels of communication through which an individual service user's voice can be heard. Equally important, however, as highlighted above, is our ability, as practitioners, to listen actively to what people tell us about their lives and to respond positively, so that we can help to make a difference to the quality of the services that service users and carers receive.

RESEARCH SUMMARY

Allan (2001) *undertook research to explore how staff can encourage people with dementia to express their views about services within everyday practice. The fieldwork was conducted with 40 practitioners, across 10 services in Scotland and England including day-centres, residential and long term-nursing homes, and lasted in some settings for six weeks and in others, as long as 10 months. The study showed that people with dementia can be meaningfully consulted about the care services that they receive even when they experience significant difficulties expressing their ideas, needs and preferences. The study highlighted that consultation should be approached in different ways using a range of verbal (for example, exchanges during intimate care, leisure or recreational activities) and non-verbal approaches (for example, using pictures, word cards or objects), as people with dementia respond to different approaches in different ways at different times. These approaches need to be developed on an individual basis, however, taking account of people's personality; their strengths, needs and preferences with regard to ways of communicating; their background and current interests; their relationship with the service that*

RESEARCH SUMMARY

they are using and their relationship with individual care practitioners. The study also high-lighted the value of providing opportunities for staff to reflect regularly on their practice, exploring different ways of consulting service users about their needs, and developing new insights and understandings about their work and their part in it. The study concluded that care staff require practical support from their organisation if they are to reflect effectively on their experience of working and communicating with people with dementia.

Formal methods such as complaints procedures and complaints advocacy are, also, some-times used to help service users and carers to express their views about, for example, the quality, cost or appropriateness of a service. When working at an individual level, it is important that we are proactive in asking service users and carers about their views on the services being provided, and that we take time to explain the complaints procedures and advocacy support services available before they need to use them (Hafford-Letchfield, 2006). Unless reassured, many people fear that complaining about services could risk retri-bution and possible service withdrawal (Simons, 1995; Crawford et al., 2003; Begum, 2006). Therefore, without the support of an independent complaints advocate, many serv-ice users and carers may fail to make a complaint. Research highlights the important role that complaints advocates provide in offering reassurance and independent advice, speak-ing on behalf of the complainant in informal settings, chasing the progress of a complaint and acting as a witness (Simons, 1995).

Approaches for collective, public decision-making

As we have seen, organisations can involve service users and carers in a range of strategic and operational decision-making forums in which there can be a trade-off between inclu-siveness and the level of control (Kirby et al., 2003a). Some formal involvement mechanisms are more suitable for use with small numbers of service users or carers, enabling them, as Kirby et al., (2003a) suggest, to have a more substantial input in public decision-making processes (for example, service development advisory groups, recruitment panels, strategic development working groups and social work programme management committees). Many local authorities, primary care trusts and NHS trusts such as the one presented in the following case study, are in the process of developing organisational structures that will support and facilitate the involvement of service users and carers in a range of decision-making processes.

CASE STUDY

Mersey Care NHS Trust aims to involve 'service users and carers in their own care and all aspects of the Trust to focus the work of the Trust on the needs of service users and carers at all times'.

The Service User and Carer Forum, which was established in 2003, comprises members from all directorates of Mersey Care including the High Secure Services, and appoints its own members to work with the Trust Board and Service Managers to improve services. To

> ### CASE STUDY *continued*
>
> date, members of the Forum have expressed their views to the Trust on a broad range of issues including:
>
> * *outpatient clinics;*
>
> * *medical staffing;*
>
> * *nursing strategy;*
>
> * *psychological services;*
>
> * *health care commission action plan;*
>
> * *model of care for adult mental health services;*
>
> * *day services for adults and older people;*
>
> * *crisis resolution and home treatment;*
>
> * *management of aggression and violence.*
>
> *At Mersey Care, over 300 service users and carers are involved in a broad range of strategic and operational decision-making forums including: the Trust Board; Service Governance Committee; contract award panels; recruitment and selection panels; policy, project and service development groups such as the Psychological Service Reference Group, and objective setting and appraisal reviews for the Trust's Senior Management Team.*
>
> *The approach adopted at Mersey Care is underpinned by a belief that service users and carers have a right, as citizens, to be involved in decisions that affect their lives. The Trust enables service users and carers to effect that right by listening and acting upon what people say to improve their experiences of the Trust's services; offering payment for people's time and providing appropriate training and support to enable service users and carers to participate in decision-making forums. For example, a diverse group of service users and carers has been recruited, trained and are supported to be involved in the recruitment and selection of Trust staff including Specialist Psychiatric Registrars (SPRs). They also participate in the selection of trainee social workers (John Moores University Social Work Degree), nursing students (Edge Hill University Mental Health Nursing programmes), and students applying for the Doctorate in Clinical Psychology at Liverpool University. Opportunities for service users in the High Secure Services to contribute to recruitment have been explored and are being piloted.*
>
> *Further information available at www.merseycare.nhs.uk/content-10*

Other more visible activities can offer opportunities for larger numbers of service users and carers to express their views and, as Kirby et al., (2003a) suggest, to influence decisions, though often with less influence over the final decision (for example, one-off or ongoing consultation exercises, satisfaction surveys, 'speaking out' suggestion boxes and evaluative research studies). In recent years, a number of publications has been produced which provide guidance on how to enable meaningful participation in a range of contexts. These guides are helpful in outlining the strengths, limitations and resource implications of a range of methods and approaches, and in providing step-by-step instructions for use. Some of the guides listed at the end of this chapter also provide practical examples that will help you to decide which methods and activities are most likely to work best for the particular initiatives with which you are involved. The next activity is designed to help you to explore some of these guides and to think about how you might use them in your future practice.

ACTIVITY **5.3**

For this activity, you should download at least one of the good practice guides listed at the end of this chapter. You might find Involving people: A practical guide, *found on the Voluntary Action Westminster website,* www.vawcvs.org/uploads/involving_people_a_practical_guide.pdf *particularly helpful.*

Read the scenarios listed below. Then, drawing on the material covered in this chapter, and the traditional and creative approaches outlined in the guides, identify what methods you could use to facilitate the involvement of service users and carers in the tasks outlined below.

1. *Staff at a residential home for older people wish to improve the planning of admissions to the home. How might they involve residents in this process?*

2. *John is white, 20 years old and has comprehension and expressive language difficulties. He recently moved to a small group home where greater emphasis is placed on promoting the quality of residents' lifestyles. How might staff facilitate John's involvement in decision-making during this period of transition?*

3. *Staff at a day centre for black people with a mental illness would like to evaluate their service provision. What approaches could be taken?*

Comment

There are several different approaches that could be taken to facilitate service user or carer participation in each of the scenarios outlined above, and no single method or approach is necessarily better than another. In tackling this exercise, you may have initially considered whether the scenarios required the involvement of one person, a small group of people or a whole community of people. In practice, the decision about how many people to involve will be determined, in part, by the nature of the task, the context, the resources available and the commitment that you are able to make. When considering your responses to each of the scenarios, you may have also thought about whether to adopt an informal or a formal approach. In scenario 1, for example, care staff could spend time getting to know new residents, informally observing and engaging in dialogue, to find out how they feel and how they have experienced their transition to the care home. Ideas and views expressed during such daily interaction could be recorded and fed upwards by front-line care staff to those who influence higher-level decisions about services and policies. Alternatively, a series of small focus groups could be established, consisting of six to 12 residents, who could share with one another not only their views of admission to the home, but also their experiences and feelings of the process. This informal approach could provide a positive, supportive social experience for residents, whilst also offering opportunities for them to take back control of their lives through facilitation of group discussions. You may have also given consideration to whole-group meetings, involving all the residents in the home. Whilst residents' meetings provide a potentially inclusive forum for involvement in decision-making about how the home is run, it is worth bearing in mind that they may not always be an appropriate forum for everyone to feel able to express their views, particularly on topics of a sensitive and confidential nature.

In contrast, you may have decided to take a more formal approach in scenario 3, for example, by involving service users as co-researchers in a piece of qualitative research, designed to obtain detailed information about their experiences of the services received. By using a simple data-collection framework, this approach encourages service users to tell their own story in their own words, and enables others to hear the voices of those who may otherwise feel inhibited about speaking up, particularly in a group setting. It would, however, be important to consult interviewers about their training and support needs, before embarking on such a project. The Mental Health Foundation, for example, supports many innovative local user-controlled research projects and provides training and support to service user researchers. Alternatively, a 'Having Your Say' consultation day could also be a good way of disseminating information, as well as consulting and evaluating a service. Such an event can attract large numbers of people with different experiences and involve staff, service users and their carers, in planning and working together over several months. It could also provide opportunities to bring together people from different groups and encourage more creative responses through the use of a variety of consultation methods, including drama, art, photography and video-making. Drama workshops, for example, which focus on what is helpful or unhelpful about a service, are a useful means of tapping the views or concerns of members of disadvantaged groups (Convention of Scottish Local Authorities, 2002) and can also be used to communicate the experiences, views and needs of the wider service user community to planners and policy-makers.

CASE STUDY

The Carers Speak Out Project, organised by The Princess Royal Trust for Carers in 2002, provided a forum for consultation with carers about their needs, priorities and issues, to inform feedback to the government about its UK Strategy for Carers. The project combined both indirect and direct consultation methods: a postal questionnaire was used to generate quantitative data on carers' issues and needs, whilst direct face-to-face consultation events, organised at a regional and national level, explored carers' views on a range of policy and service issues. In planning these events, The Princess Royal Trust for Carers Centres was encouraged to try out different and creative ideas in consultation. In consequence, whilst many of the consultation events and conferences contained structured workshops or discussion groups to gather and record carers' views, organisers tried to avoid running their events in a 'traditional' format. The consultation event held at Moray, for example, was combined with an Information Fair, which provided information on services of benefit to carers and gave feedback on previous consultations through the use of posters and a drama performance. Some consultation events provided additional informative activities including relaxation sessions, aromatherapy, reflexology, massage, sessions covering soft furnishing, floristry or art and craft, so that the day was enjoyable as well as productive. In Wandsworth, a different style of event was run, providing opportunities for carers to express their views in different ways. Drama sessions, for example, were used as a consultation method and a graphic artist recorded carers' views in pictures.

(Keeley and Clarke, 2003)

As we have seen already, it is important to respect people's rights to make choices about the ways in which they are involved, and to ensure that there are supports and structures in place to enable them to participate whenever and however they wish (Evans and Banton, 2001). This is important for service users and carers, regardless of whether they participate in decision-making that directly affects their own lives or impacts more widely on the lives of others. Whilst involvement has been hard to achieve for many groups of service users, as highlighted in Chapters 1 and 3, there are particular issues and challenges involved in facilitating the inclusion of people with complex needs (Clare and Cox, 2003). Young people who have a learning disability, like John in scenario 2 in Activity 5.3, need to be encouraged to express their views about the choices available to them, particularly at times of transition. The choices for this group of service users can often be limited, presenting difficulties for staff about how to ensure that individuals' voices are heard in decision-making processes, particularly when, like John, they also have a communication impairment (Cameron and Murphy, 2002). Research suggests that augmentative communication systems can be used successfully at such times, to encourage interaction and conversation and to facilitate involvement in life planning (Cameron and Murphy, 2002). In John's case, staff could use pictorial symbols to augment his existing ways of communicating, so that John can indicate his likes and dislikes and express his views about the leisure and recreational choices available to him. It would also be important in John's case, to consider how his contribution could be strengthened further by, for example, using this framework to facilitate his views at future needs meetings or reviews.

C H A P T E R   S U M M A R Y

This chapter has explored some of the practical ways of encouraging and facilitating the involvement and participation of adult service users and carers in social work practice. As we have seen, building and sustaining participatory practice is dependent upon three main variables: the establishment of an organisational culture and infrastructure that support participation; the development of strong, positive relationships between social workers, service users and carers; and the provision of effective practical and emotional support mechanisms for service users and carers. Each of these aspects takes time to develop and it is important, therefore, that you are realistic about what can be achieved in a given situation. It takes time to build infrastructures and to change people's attitudes; to establish trust and to develop mutual respect; and for people who may be unused to participating, it takes time to develop the confidence and skills needed to be involved (CCNAP, 2001).

In this chapter, we have placed particular emphasis on developing an approach to involvement that encompasses a range of methods and activities, and have examined some of the traditional and innovative activities used in everyday practice to involve service users and carers in different types of decision-making processes. Arguably, more important, however, is the actual approach that you take to involving service users and carers in your work. For us, participation is a way of working that derives from a genuine and positive approach that respects and values the expertise that service users and carers contribute. Placing individual service users and carers at the centre of the participatory process and treating them as equal partners by involving them in choosing appropriate methods or tools for the task are important, therefore, in giving them ownership of that process. In the next chapter, we will turn our attention to how we can work in partnership with children and young people to create 'listening spaces' (Children's Rights Officers and Advocates, 2000) where their voices can be heard, and their views taken seriously about the way that services are planned, delivered and evaluated.

Convention of Scottish Local Authorities (COSLA) (2002) *Focusing on citizens: A guide to approaches and methods.* **www.dundeecity.gov.uk/ce**

This detailed guidance outlines a range of innovative methods and approaches to encourage councils and other public bodies to look at new ways of involving the public in decision-making processes.

Department of Health (DoH) (2006) *Reward and recognition: the principles and practice of service user payment and reimbursement in health and social care. A guide for service providers, service users and carers*, 2nd edn. London: Department of Health.

This best-practice guide aims to support local health and social care organisations with the principles and practice of reimbursing and paying service users for their involvement.

Keeley, B and Clarke, M (2001) *Consultation with carers. Good practice guide.* **www.carers.org/data/files/consultation-9.pdf**

A comprehensive guide on how to consult carers based on the Carers Speak Out Project undertaken by the Princess Royal Trust for Carers in 2002. It provides a useful checklist for planning and running a consultation event and identifies the general principles underpinning successful consultation.

Simons, K (1999) *A place at the table? Involving people with learning difficulties in purchasing and commissioning services.* Kidderminster: British Institute of Learning Disabilities.

This book explores how to encourage and support the participation of people with a learning difficulty in the purchasing and commissioning of services.

Terence Higgins Trust (2002) *Practice guidance on involving people with HIV and other long term conditions in planning and developing services.* **www.tht.org.uk/informationresources/ publications/policyreports/practiceguidancedevelopingservices.pdf**

A brief practice guide to increasing and supporting the involvement of people with HIV in statutory and consultative structures. Contains some helpful case studies illustrating key methods and issues.

Voluntary Action Westminster (2006) *Involving people: A practical guide.* **www.vawcvs.org/uploads/involving_people_a_practical_guide.pdf**

A useful practical guide to involvement for all front-line staff and managers of public services which focuses on choosing and implementing the most appropriate method. A helpful table provides an overview of the best methods to use for different situations.

Chapter 6

Participation in practice: involving children

ACHIEVING A SOCIAL WORK DEGREE

This chapter will help you to meet the following National Occupational Standards:

Key Role 1: Prepare for, and work with individuals, families, carers, groups and communities to assess their needs and circumstances.
- Work with individuals, families, carers, groups and communities to help them make informed decisions.
- Assess needs and options to recommend a course of action.

Key Role 2: Plan, carry out, review and evaluate social work practice, with individuals, families, carers, groups, communities and other professionals.
- Interact with individuals, families, carers, groups and communities to achieve change and development and to improve life opportunities.
- Prepare, produce, implement and evaluate plans with individuals, families, carers, groups, communities and professional colleagues.
- Work with groups to promote individual growth, development and independence.

Key Role 3: Support individuals to represent their needs, views and circumstances.
- Advocate with, and on behalf of, individuals, families, carers, groups and communities.
- Prepare for, and participate in decision-making forums.

Key Role 5: Manage and be accountable, with supervision and support, for your own social work practice within your organisation.
- Contribute to the management of resources and services.

Key Role 6: Demonstrate professional competence in social work practice.
- Research, analyse, evaluate, and use current knowledge of best social work practice.
- Work within agreed standards of social work practice and ensure own professional development.

It will also introduce you to the following academic standards as set out in the social work subject benchmark statements:

2.4 Defining principles
- Help people to gain, regain or maintain control of their own affairs, insofar as this is compatible with their own or others' safety, well-being and rights.

3.1.3 Values and ethics
- The nature, historical evolution and application of social work values.

3.1.4 Social work theory
- Research-based concepts and critical explanations from social work theory and other disciplines that contribute to the knowledge base of social work.
- Approaches and methods of intervention in a range of community-based settings including group-care at individual, group and community levels, including factors guiding the choice and evaluation of these.

3.1.5 The nature of social work practice
- The characteristics of practice in a range of community-based and organisational settings including group-care, within statutory, voluntary and private sectors, and the factors influencing changes in practice within these contexts.
- The nature and characteristics of skills associated with effective practice, both direct and indirect, with a range of service users and in a variety of settings including group-care.

- The place of theoretical perspectives and evidence from international research in assessment and decision-making processes in social work practice.
- The integration of theoretical perspectives and evidence from international research into the design and implementation of effective social work intervention with a wide range of service users, carers and others.
- The processes of reflection and evaluation, including familiarity with the range of approaches for evaluating welfare outcomes, and their significance for the development of practice and the practitioner.

The subject skills highlighted to demonstrate this knowledge in practice include:

3.2.2 Problem-solving skills

3.2.2.1 Managing problem-solving activities.

3.2.2.2 Gathering information.

3.2.2.3 Analysis and synthesis.

3.2.2.4 Intervention and evaluation.

3.2.3 Communication skills

- Listen actively to others, engage appropriately with the life experiences of service users, understand accurately their viewpoint and overcome personal prejudices to respond appropriately to a range of complex personal and interpersonal situations.
- Use both verbal and non-verbal cues to guide interpretation.
- Identify and use opportunities for purposeful and supportive communication with service users within their everyday living situations.
- Communicate effectively across potential barriers resulting from differences.

3.2.4 Skills in working with others

- Involve users of social work services in ways that increase their resources, capacity and power to influence factors affecting their lives.
- Consult actively with others, including service users, who hold relevant information or expertise.
- Act co-operatively with others, liaising and negotiating across differences such as organisational and professional boundaries and differences of identity or language.
- Develop effective helping relationships and partnerships with other individuals, groups and organisations that facilitate change.
- Challenge others when necessary, in ways that are most likely to produce positive outcomes.

Introduction

The participation of children and young people in social work policy and practice is a relatively new phenomenon. For many years, adult interpretations of children's wishes and needs have determined services and influenced research and policy (Franklin and Sloper, 2004). Although over the past 30 years, there has been a slow but growing recognition in policy and practice of the need to involve children and young people in decision-making processes, research suggests that the amount of work undertaken by statutory and voluntary agencies to involve children and young people in public decision-making processes has only really increased since 2000 (Oldfield and Fowler, 2004).

As we saw in Chapter 2, new thinking about children and young people's participation is now central to the current government legislative, policy and guidance framework underpinning the delivery of public services to children and young people. This new thinking has been influenced by a number of parallel social and political changes at national and international level:

- *The changing views of childhood* – over time, academic research has challenged the views held of childhood as simply a period of socialisation in which children are rarely asked for their own opinions or views. Research (see, for example, Alderson, 1993) has helped to increase our understanding of children's competencies to participate in decision-making, and children and young people have become increasingly identified as a group in their own right (Franklin and Sloper, 2004).

- *The emergence of the children's rights agenda* – children and young people began to gain legal participatory rights in decision-making under the UN Convention on the Rights of the Child (UNCRC), ratified in the UK in 1991. This helped to focus adult thinking on how best to involve children and young people in decision-making processes that were *appropriate to their abilities and understanding* (Franklin and Sloper, 2004, p6).

- *The increasing influence of the consumer* – children and young people, as consumers, were given more power (through legislation and policy) to exercise choice and influence the nature and quality of the services that they received (Franklin and Sloper, 2004).

- *The impact of high-profile child-protection cases* – a series of UK public inquiries in the late 1980s and early 1990s, which documented widespread systematic physical and sexual abuse by staff in children's homes led to an acknowledgement that traditional attitudes towards children, based on the view that 'adults know best' and act in children's best interests, had failed many children (Lansdown, 2001). It was recognised that, *surrounded by a culture of collusion, neglect, indifference and silence on the part of staff* (Lansdown, 2001, p3), many children were being denied a voice. 'Speaking with', 'listening to' and actively involving children could more readily ensure their protection (Scottish Executive, 2004).

- *The emergence of children's service user and carer movements* – a range of groups has emerged such as the Children's Rights Alliance for England; the Children's Society National Young Carers Initiative and A National Voice, who campaign to transform the lives and status of children and young people in the UK.

In consequence, children and young people's participation in the UK has moved a long way in a relatively short space of time (Franklin and Sloper, 2004). However, although *social care organisations have begun to acknowledge that, when listened to, children and young people can play a vital role in the planning and delivery of services* (Wright et al., 2006, p4), there is still some way to go if children and young people are to be able to exercise greater choice and power in both individual and collective decision-making processes. The challenge for us as social workers, therefore, is to assess how best to do this.

In this chapter, we will start by examining some of the specific issues surrounding the participation of children and young people in social work practice, and explore the social worker's role in challenging commonly-held perceptions of some groups of children and young people. We will then explore some of the fears that can be felt by practitioners regarding the involvement of children and young people, and examine some of the challenges facing the social worker in learning to adopt appropriate support roles. There will be opportunities to identify the key skills that are required of practitioners in enabling the participation of children and young people both in collective and individual decision-making processes, and there will also be opportunities to reflect on the implications of this for your own future practice. In the final part of the chapter, we will consider some of the approaches that can be employed in working with children and young people to create 'listening spaces' (CROA, 2000) or 'participatory spaces' (Marchant and Kirby, 2004) in which children and young people can have a meaningful say.

Involving children and young people

Participatory work with children and young people requires that adults create accepting environments where children's voices can be heard, and their views taken seriously about the way that services are planned, delivered and evaluated. Historically, the power relations between children and adults in consultations and other participatory opportunities have mirrored wider societal power relations and differences (Marchant and Kirby, 2004) based on factors such as age, gender, race/ethnicity, culture, disability, sexuality, class and poverty. This has resulted in specific groups of children and young people becoming more marginalised in participatory work than others, as can be seen in Figure 6.1.

Figure 6.1 Groups of children and young people who are often marginalised
(Franklin and Sloper, 2004; Oldfield and Fowler, 2004; Wright and Haydon, 2002, cited in Wright et al., 2006)

The challenge for social workers is to find ways to reduce these power imbalances through good practice. In essence, enabling children and young people to exercise greater choice, control and power demands that we find ways of:

- changing existing relationships between adults and children;
- countering discriminatory and oppressive practices;
- involving children more fully in individual and collective decision-making processes.

As we have seen, children and young people, like adult service users and carers, are not a homogenous group: they are all different, and are able to participate in different ways, at different ages and to different degrees (Beresford and Croft, 1993). The way that children and young people are perceived, however, can facilitate or hinder their participation (Marchant and Kirby, 2004) in the decision-making processes that affect their lives. The next activity will help you to think about the different ways in which children and young people may be viewed, and to consider the implications of this for your own practice.

ACTIVITY **6.1**

What factors would you take into consideration when ascertaining the views of the following service users?

- *15-month-old boy of dual heritage who has been removed from his mother's care;*

- *a 5-year-old boy with cerebral palsy;*

- *a 10-year-old Asian girl who is looking after her father following a road traffic accident;*

- *a white 16-year-old mother of twins.*

How might these factors influence your approach when working with these children and young people?

Comment

Thinking about the differences between individual children and young people makes us look at the way that we perceive and treat young service users and carers more generally. Some of the assumptions that mitigate against children and young people's involvement and participation include beliefs that they are:

- incompetent, irresponsible or unreliable;

- vulnerable and in need of care and protection;

- egocentric, thinking only of themselves;

- 'developing adults' in which childhood is a training ground for adulthood;

- ready to take full responsibility for controlling their own lives.

(Lansdown, 2001; Marchant and Kirby, 2004; Wright et al., 2006)

When you started to think about the above activity, one of your first thoughts may have been the need to assess each individual's level of competence to participate. Although levels of competence are determined in part by visible factors such as age and disability, if you believe that everyone, including babies and very young children, can express their feelings and preferences, then you will have approached this activity from the standpoint that each child and young person has the capacity to be involved in decision-making processes about their own lives. From this viewpoint, ascertaining an individual's views, whether they are a baby or a teenager, means being able to understand how they 'see' or perceive the world, and to understand their feelings about their experiences (Marchant and Kirby,

2004). We all develop opinions and ideas about the world around us, based on our lived experiences. This includes babies and younger children who, arguably, know most about how they feel and how they experience their own lives (Marchant and Kirby, 2004). If you have ever observed a mother try to wean her seven-month-old baby onto solid food, for example, you will know how quickly babies can develop likes and dislikes for certain foods, and convey these feelings through body sounds, facial expressions and gestures to show approval or disapproval. Therefore, as Marchant and Kirby (2004) note, even very young children can offer us unique insights into their world, provided that we are willing to observe, to listen and to hear what they tell us.

Theories and explanations of human development suggest that children develop greater independence and capabilities as they get older (Crawford and Walker, 2003), but that they also *develop at different rates and are influenced by a range of factors specific to their individual circumstances* (Wright et al., 2006, p30). For this reason, it is important that each child or young person is involved in ways that are appropriate for them, given their abilities, experience and interests. Therefore, whilst it might be easier and quicker in assessments, for example, for professionals to gather information from parents of young children or children with complex needs, it is important that these children do not become marginalised. Evidence from research and practice highlights the importance of offering children of all ages a range of ways to participate (Wright et al., 2006). Identifying children's individuals needs for participation and adopting a range of creative and flexible approaches (Franklin and Sloper, 2004) are important, therefore, in promoting the participation rights of all children and young people.

Arguably, of all the groups of service users and carers, children and young people are perhaps the most vulnerable to being talked about over their heads, or having their opinions ignored because of the general imbalance in power between children and adults in our society. Such experiences can often inhibit or check the development of children and young people's competence to say how they feel (Marchant and Kirby, 2004). Experience of being listened to and of participating in decision-making processes will vary from child to child, and will be influenced by a number of factors, including their family composition and wider culture, their place in the family and their age. Some children whose feelings, needs and opinions in the past have been ignored or misinterpreted, may believe that their voices will be automatically silenced or misunderstood; others may have never learned to share their feelings or emotions (Bannister, 2001). Inevitably, this will affect the confidence and capacity of some children and young people to express their views about their needs and the ways in which these can be met. It is important, therefore, that all children and young people are provided with genuine participatory opportunities that help them to develop their confidence and belief that social workers want to hear what they really think and feel. It is also important that as practitioners, we make the time to develop relationships in which children and young people's views are genuinely respected, and listened to (Marchant and Kirby, 2004). Children need reassurance that there are no right or wrong answers (Marchant and Kirby, 2004), that they can change their minds about what they have said and that they will not be punished for their opinions (Bannister, 2001). This is particularly important where children may feel that they are held responsible for the difficulties that exist in their family, or where they have had to seek asylum or have experience as refugees.

RESEARCH SUMMARY

Tom is 10 years old and looked after by the local authority. He is a quiet, shy boy who has been in care since the age of seven. During this time, he has experienced five different placements and is currently living in a children's home, following the sudden death of his foster carer in a road traffic accident. Tom talks of being known as a number on a file. His social worker never has the time to speak to him and he has no proper understanding about the reasons for his removal from home or why his mum is not allowed to see him. He states that his review meetings are a waste of time. He can never get a word in because everyone who attends think that they know what he wants and don't give him a chance to have a say. 'They just tell me what will happen, and even when I do say what I want, it never happens, so there's no point really saying anything.'

Service user and carer involvement and participation in social work practice present opportunities for mutual learning; learning, however, requires humility on our part, an ability to listen and a willingness to reflect on our relationships with children and young people (Marchant and Kirby, 2004). It is important to start to begin this process of self-reflection and awareness-raising before you start to work with children and young people. The next activity will provide opportunities for you to reflect on how your learning from this chapter so far will help to develop your own professional practice.

ACTIVITY 6.2

It is important to become more aware of how you think and feel about issues, how you present to children and young people and what messages you may convey in your relations with them. Think for a moment about the implications of your learning so far in this chapter. How might your learning inform your future work with children and young people? Choose a colleague or friend and ask if you could share your learning with them.

Comment

This activity is not easy and demands a willingness to be honest and open with ourselves and with others – key personal qualities required when working with service users and carers. We suggest that you consider the following key points in relation to your own future work with children and young people.

- Be ready to challenge your own, and others' assumptions and prejudices about children's capabilities and their roles in society (Marchant and Kirby, 2004). Actually facilitating children and young people's participation will help to challenge other people's attitudes by questioning their underlying values and assumptions about children (Boyden and Ennew, 1997, cited in Marchant and Kirby, 2004).

- Try to adopt an approach that sees children and young people as participants who are comparable to adults, whilst at the same time understanding that they require special consideration because:

- their competencies are different, not less than adults';

- they are potentially vulnerable.

This means that children and young people may require information, training, resources and support to understand the options and consequences of making choices (Marchant and Kirby, 2004) and to ensure that participation is a positive experience (Wright et al., 2006).

- Be aware that each child or young person needs to be involved in ways that are appropriate to their age and understanding, their past experiences, abilities and interests. This means that you will need to develop awareness of, and be able to respond to, the wider developmental and cultural factors that impact on children and young people's competence and capacity to participate (Marchant and Kirby, 2004).

- Be aware that children and young people can choose whether to participate or not. Provide adequate and relevant information so that they can give their informed consent to participate (Wright et al., 2006) alongside any adults who may need to give their consent such as parents or carers.

- Take time to build rapport so that children and young people gain trust, feel understood and feel accepted (Bannister, 2001).

- Try to develop a range of approaches and use different skills according to each child's competencies. This will require particular awareness of the barriers that disabled children and young people face, so that you can ensure that you provide adequate time, support and resources to enable these to be overcome (Wright et al., 2006).

Challenges of supporting and sustaining participation

No one will tell you that participatory work with children and young people is easy. However, if you hold a genuine belief that children's feelings and understanding of their situation are of equal value to those of adults, then you will feel committed to ensuring that their voices are heard in all decision-making processes that affect their lives. Before we move on to think about the challenges that face you in learning to adopt appropriate support roles and in thinking about the skills that you will need to engage children and young people, we would like to invite you to participate in an activity that will help you to think about any worries or fears that you may have about participatory work. When introducing children and young people to the idea of participation, it can be helpful to offer them a range of practical activities that provide them with opportunities to think about how they feel, and to explore any aspects that might be worrying them. There are many hands-on activities, such as the one described below, that can be used for this purpose.

ACTIVITY 6.3

The mighty oak

The oak has become an iconic symbol of the British landscape. For many generations, this tree has been revered as a source of personal strength and spiritual renewal, enabling those who sit beneath its unfaltering boughs to find new insight and understanding, and to develop courage and resolution.

For this activity, which you may like to undertake with a colleague or friend, you will need a large sheet of white paper, six pieces of A4 card in autumn shades (for example, brown, orange, burgundy, yellow), a piece of tracing or greaseproof paper, a pair of scissors, a brown marker pen, a black felt tip pen and some reusable adhesive.

Draw a large oak tree in the centre of your white paper – it will need to have a strong, majestic trunk and a crown of twisted branches. Then, draw three leaves of differing sizes – small, medium and large – onto tracing paper and trace the outline of each leaf several times onto different pieces of coloured card. Cut the leaves out and group them in piles according to their size.

Then, think of any worries or fears that you may have about participatory work with children or young people. Write each of these onto a leaf. Some of your worries may feel really big to you and we would like you to write these on the larger leaves, reserving the smaller leaves for the issues that worry you least. Position each leaf onto your oak tree. If you are working with a friend or colleague, you may wish to share your thoughts and feelings evoked by this activity.

Comment

This activity can provide a focus for future discussion and exploration of personal learning. It may be a useful tool in personal action planning, particularly in helping you to identify some of your own practice learning needs. As you engage in participatory work, your confidence will grow, and many of the worries or fears that you identified initially will fade. You may find it helpful to revisit your oak tree regularly so that you can remind yourself of your progress, and collect the leaves off your tree, rather like a gardener gathers fallen leaves in autumn. As you may know, mulching or composting provides organic matter that, over time, helps to enrich the soil. Similarly, identifying your worries about participation and putting plans in place that will help you to overcome these fears, will ensure that your confidence grows, that your competence increases and that your practice with service users and carers becomes greatly enriched.

As we have seen in Chapter 2, social workers are now legally required to involve all children and young people in decisions that affect their lives. This can include helping a child to participate in decisions in person, for example, at a meeting or through a telephone or video link, or advocating on behalf of a child when decisions need to be made that will affect them, by drawing on evidence from the child's writings such as a letter or diary, a tape-recording or drawings. You may have found the above activity challenging, particularly if you have not had many opportunities to engage with children of different ages, and may have particular worries about 'getting it wrong'. This is not unusual, and is a worry shared by some qualified social workers with many years of social work experience. Being humble, accepting that we are not experts and being ready to learn from children and young people, however, is the first step to being able to see the world from the child's perspective (Marchant and Kirby, 2004). In this sense, adult modesty can be seen as a powerful weapon in empowering children and young people (Delfos, 2001, cited in Marchant and Kirby, 2004, p140).

Other worries that social workers often have include:

- not having the special expertise to talk with particular groups of children and young people such as those who are very young or have a disability;

- not knowing what activities to use or how to deal with sensitive issues;

- appearing to be different or to be doing things differently from others in the team;

- not being taken seriously or listened to by other staff, including managers;

- not having sufficient time to work with children and young people;

- not having access to sufficient resources because of budget constraints.

Much of the time, involving children and young people is about adapting our own ways of communicating, so that we can develop new ways of working that are child-friendly and responsive to children's needs and agendas. Many organisations now provide initial induction and ongoing training opportunities for staff at all levels to help to prepare them for participatory work. Inevitably, as with any change process, you may meet resistance and conflict between old and new ways of working within your social work team. This may require that you *challenge staff whose attitudes or behaviour are harmful*, or that you *work around those who will not change* (Kirby et al., 2003b, p38). Moreover, supervision and staff meetings provide opportunities and forums to encourage the discussion of practice so that any barriers to participation can be overcome. Building partnerships with other agencies where specific support mechanisms are in place for participation can also help to develop your own capacity to work in participatory ways.

Skills for effective participation

As Marchant and Kirby observe:

> *Commentators too often focus on children's competence to participate rather than on adults' competence to support children to make decisions and take action.*

> (Marchant and Kirby, 2004, p136)

All social workers working with children and young people need to learn to adopt *appropriate support roles* (Marchant and Kirby, 2004, p136), and to develop a range of skills that will enable the participation of children and young people in both collective and individual decision-making processes. Whilst you will already be using many of the skills required in your day-to-day life, you may need to be prepared to adapt how you use these skills to ensure that your approach is child-friendly. The next activity will help you to identify some of the key skills needed to implement and enable the involvement of children and young people in your work, and will provide you with opportunities to reflect on your own specific learning and development needs in relation to participation.

ACTIVITY 6.4

Butterfly collage

For this activity, you will need a large sheet of flipchart paper, several sheets of A4 brightly coloured paper, a variety of craft materials (for example, scraps of fabric, buttons, wool, etc.), a pack of gold star stickers, coloured felt tip pens, glue, and a pair of scissors.

On flipchart paper, draw an outline of a large butterfly and cut out small shapes of brightly coloured paper, sufficiently large to take written words or phrases. Then identify the skills that you think are required for participatory work with children and young people, and write each skill on a separate coloured shape. Using the craft materials, create a butterfly collage, and integrate your coloured shapes on to your butterfly's wings.

When you have completed your collage, mark the participation skills that you feel you already have with a gold star. These may be skills that you have developed through personal or professional contact with children and young people, or they may be skills that you use with adult service users and carers that you feel are transferable to your social work practice with children and young people. Then note down which skills you feel less confident about. You may like to share this part of the activity with a colleague or friend by asking them to help you to reflect on what you have learnt from this exercise about yourself, and how your learning can inform your future practice with children and young people.

Comment

In order to work effectively with children and young people, we have to be prepared to try out new ways of working. You may have found the last two hands-on activities fun and creative, or you may have found them quite a challenging task. Certainly, working with children and young people requires us to let go of our adult assumptions about ways of doing things. This means that we have to be prepared to take risks. It also requires that we show flexibility by encouraging children to influence the direction of the work. Like adult service users and carers, children and young people have their own agendas, their views about what should happen and their own ideas about how this should happen. We need to be responsive to this.

In considering the key participatory skills required by social workers when working with children and young people, you may have identified some of the skills listed in Figure 6.2.

Figure 6.2 Key participation skills
(*Source*: CATS and YIPPEE, 2002; Marchant and Kirby, 2004)

In undertaking Activity 6.4, you may have noticed that involving children and young people in social work practice requires many of the same skills that are used in participatory work with adult service users and carers. It is important to recognise, however, that you will need to adapt the way that you use these skills, so that your practice becomes tailored to each child's needs and understanding. Observing, listening and communicating with children and young people are central to participatory work – we cannot possibly know what a child is thinking or feeling unless they tell us (Marchant and Kirby, 2004). Children and young people communicate their emotions, opinions and views in a variety of different ways, for example, through talking, through their behaviour, through gestures and sounds, through play, and through art, music and dance. Observing children's behaviour and interactions with adults, siblings and peers, therefore, can be helpful in learning about the different ways in which they communicate their feelings, needs and opinions, and in assessing the quality of their relationships (Adcock, 2001). This is particularly important where children communicate without speech, as in the case of very young children or those with a disability. Listening to children is, however, much more than simply hearing what they tell us. It is also about indicating to them that we have heard what has been said (Thompson, 1996). Active listening requires giving attention; mirroring body postures to facilitate trust and to communicate equality and respect (Bannister, 2001); resisting interrupting and jumping to conclusions; acknowledging feelings and reflecting back what has been said through paraphrasing to confirm understanding (Thompson, 1996). Demonstrating that we value what has been said requires that we take the time to listen, for as Thompson acknowledges, the skills of listening are *intertwined with time management skills* (1996, p85). Moreover, to communicate effectively with children, we need to ensure that we use uncomplicated sentences that avoid jargon; speak at the child's pace, stressing key words (Marchant and Kirby, 2004) and convey warmth, respect and interest through the tone in our voices. Where children have complex needs, it is important that we use communication methods that are appropriate to their individual needs (such as gestures, signs, symbols and pictures), and that we also seek out people who can assist us to communicate with them (such as interpreters and signers) (Marchant, 2001).

In thinking about the development of your own participatory skills, it is important that you become aware of your own mode of communicating, so that you can identify any language or behaviours that might restrict or silence children's voices, or show a lack of regard for them. Thinking about how you might explain who you are and what your role is to children and young people of different ages can be a good way of checking whether the language that you use is uncomplicated and jargon-free. It can also help you to think about the tools that you might employ to ensure that your approach is child-friendly. A small photograph album depicting pictures of the work that you do at the office, in meetings, visiting parents or playing with children in their homes, for example, can help to place you in your professional context (Brandon, Schofield and Trinder, 1998).

There are many stresses and conflicts within the social work role (Shardlow and Nelson, 2005) and you are likely to encounter situations where, having listened to what children tell you, you find yourself needing to negotiate between them and your manager. As Shardlow and Nelson (2005, p18) observe, challenging others *does not require aggression, but the positive use of assertiveness*, so that you are able to advocate on behalf of children and young people, particularly if your manager is blocking your requests due to resource constraints. In such contexts, resource-gathering skills can be important in offering service users full information and alternative resources that are available in their local area (CATS and YIPPEE, 2002).

CASE STUDY

Since 2003, the Service User and Carer Involvement Project, based in the Department of Social Work and Social Care at Anglia Ruskin University, has organised a series of 'information fairs' in which a variety of service user and carer organisations run 'stalls' aimed at increasing student awareness and understanding of their services. Feedback suggests that these events are highly valued among students, partner agencies and staff, enabling them to network, to learn about local resources and to learn more directly from the people who use and run these organisations. These information fairs also provide opportunities to forge partnerships and to develop more effective working relationships with service users, carers and their organisations.

Reflecting honestly on our work and being able to accept criticism or suggestions from children and young people about how we can improve services are also important. As we have seen, providing service users and carers with feedback to let them know the outcomes of their involvement helps to validate their contributions and to affirm that their views have been heard and responded to. When feeding back, however, it is important to do so in ways that make sense to children and young people, using methods that are child-friendly. This can be done either verbally or in written form, or a combination of both, and can draw on materials provided by the children and young people themselves such as artwork or taped discussions to illustrate particular points.

RESEARCH SUMMARY

Kirwan, Aubrey and Moules (2004) *were commissioned by the Children's Fund Essex to undertake an evaluation of the non-use of services by children, young people and families. As part of this research, nine children were trained in research methods, data collection and analysis with a view to them conducting research to find out why children and young people aged 5–15 years didn't use the clubs and groups that were provided within their local communities. The Research Team of Young People produced a colourful child-friendly report containing clear text, photographs and artwork to disseminate their findings to other children and young people, and were also involved in the delivery of a presentation of their findings at the National Children's Bureau Conference in London.*

As part of the research synopsis, the Research Team of Young People produced a checklist of the skills that they felt adults needed to work with children and young people. These were:

- *ask children and young people what they want to do rather than just guess;*

- *patience – give them a chance to respond;*

- *co-operative – listen and try to understand what they are saying;*

- *treat everyone fairly;*

- *don't force children and young people to join in with games or anything else;*

- *have fun.*

Approaches to participation

As we have seen, it is important for children and young people to be given space to:

- *make their own decisions;*

- *develop their own strategies;*

- *define their own agenda;*

- *access information;*

- *speak for themselves.*

(Sketchley and Walker, 2001, p2).

Given children and young people's differing levels of competence, it is important that we are creative about developing participatory opportunities that enable all children to communicate what they think and feel (Marchant and Kirby, 2004). As Marchant and Kirby (2004, p148) observe, approaches to the involvement of children and young people need to be *engaging, stimulating and fun.* In this final section of the chapter, therefore, we will explore a range of creative, child-centred approaches to participation.

As we have seen already, the methods and approaches to the involvement of service users and carers need to be informed by the context in which participation is sought, whether this be, for example, with regard to service development and provision; research or in policy development. Children and young people's participation can be for themselves as an individual, or collectively on behalf of a group or groups of children and young people, with opportunities for involvement at three different levels, as shown in Figure 6.3.

Figure 6.3 Levels of children and young people's participation

The next activity will provide opportunities for you to explore each level of participation.

ACTIVITY *6.5*

Draw a table with three columns and head the columns: individual level, group level and national level. Then think of examples to illustrate children and young people's involvement in decision-making at each of the three levels.

Comment

The types of personal decisions that children and young people can participate in vary and can include: consent to participate; decisions about their leisure and play activities; decisions about their learning, health treatment and care support, and decisions relating to child protection and family law proceedings (Kirby et al., 2003a). When working with children and young people, your approach will be determined in part by the purpose and likely length of the work, the nature of your relationship with the child or young person, and the child's interests and abilities, racial, religious and cultural background (Brandon et al., 1998). A range of guides and resource packs is now available to support the participation of children and young people in personal decision-making processes. These packs provide a plethora of creative, activity-based communication tools that can help you to listen to children and young people, and help them to communicate with you. It is important to bear in mind that you will need to adapt and fit such resources and techniques to each individual child's cognitive and intellectual ability, emotional maturity and personal circumstances (Brandon et al., 1998).

When using such resources, it is important not to impose your materials on a child or young person, but to use them to negotiate how you will spend your time together (Brandon et al., 1998). Brandon et al. (1998) provide ideas about the use of a 'kit-bag' containing materials, such as puppets, modelling clay, play people and drawing materials including collage items, to help children of different ages to express their wishes and feelings. Visual methods can be particularly useful in engaging young children, but it is important not to make assumptions that all young children require such props to express themselves, when they can capably do so verbally (Marchant and Kirby, 2004). In contrast, whilst many adolescents may feel more comfortable chatting with you, it is important to offer them a choice of materials and opportunities for 'playing' (Brandon et al., 1998) – for some young people this can prove a cathartic process. Using techniques such as eco-mapping, timelines and diaries can help children and young people to share relevant information with you and plan for the future. The next activity will introduce you to a timeline resource that can provide an excellent basis for a discussion with a child or young person about their relationships, and the changes that they have experienced in their life.

ACTIVITY 6.6

The river of life

Social workers are often involved in helping children and young people to make life-changing decisions or plans. This can sometimes involve moving them from one home to another or supporting them to leave school or to become a parent. Understanding the impacts of grief, loss and change are central to our understanding of a child's wishes and feelings about the future.

Try to undertake this activity with a friend or colleague. Using felt tip pens, ask your partner to draw their 'river of life' on a large sheet of flipchart paper, charting key changes or turning points in their life with regard to accommodation, family relationships, education, health, and work. Intersperse drawing with talking and listening, letting your colleague guide the conversation as they reflect on their life.

Afterwards, identify the pros and cons of using this technique.

Ensuring that children and young people have access to appropriate communication methods and imaginative and creative techniques, can make a significant difference to how they experience participatory processes. With this in mind, the Department for Education and Skills commissioned Barnardo's to develop a resource pack to support practitioners in conducting assessments and drawing up care plans (Hutton and Partridge, 2006). The pack consists of a printed guide and CD-ROM of practical resources which use different media such as art, play, drama and music, to help children reflect on their experiences, feelings, wishes, and support networks. Similarly, Save the Children (Shephard and Treseder, 2002) have produced a resource pack of tried-and-tested activities for use in gathering information, long-term planning and evaluation. The activities in this pack can be used in both individual and collective decision-making processes. Details of these resources can be found at the end of this chapter.

In thinking about Activity 6.5, you may have identified the potential for children and young people to participate in many types of strategic and operational decision-making tasks at a group level through, for example, youth forums, advisory and reference groups, or creative youth groups. Such mechanisms for involving children and young people in public decision-making operate in various ways, with different degrees of decision-making power and autonomy (Kirby et al., 2003a). The important task for you as a social worker, however, will be to tailor the type of group to the particular issue under consideration and the outcomes being sought. Some groups, for example, may be set up as isolated consultation events that are responsive to adult concerns and agendas (Kirby et al., 2003a). Other groups that are ongoing may focus on developing more autonomous spaces where children and young people have opportunities to plan and manage their own projects. The current emphasis within many organisations where there is a commitment to children's participation, is on the development of participatory support groups, where children and young people are supported by adults workers, such as Local Authority Children's Participation Officers, to identify their own issues of concern and to take action. Such groups are often linked into existing structures, so that children and young people's views can be passed on to relevant adult decision-makers (Kirby et al., 2003a), as illustrated in the case example below.

CASE STUDY

Cambridge Children's Services support four groups of children and young people who have experience of being looked after in foster, residential or leaving care services. The 'Just Us' groups provide opportunities for children and young people aged 8–20 years to meet for an hour-and-a-half each month in four locations across the county to chat with mates, to engage in discussions and the creative arts including drama, and to have fun together. Structures are in place for these groups of children and young people to feed back their views and opinions, and to influence service-delivery and development. For example, the group has been involved in designing the Children's Services Looked After Children Manual on how reviews should be implemented. This has led to young people:

- *no longer being sent letters inviting them to their own home for a review meeting;*
- *being more involved in the planning of reviews with regard to who is invited and where the review is held;*
- *chairing their own reviews.*

'Just Us' have also participated in a 'Question Time' project providing opportunities to put questions to senior managers and councillors. They drew up an action plan and prioritised the proposed changes. The changes that were agreed included:

- *the provision of a laptop for all looked-after young people at Key Stage 4;*
- *young people's attendance at the fostering panel;*
- *young people giving feedback on foster carers' reviews.*

The 'Just Us' group has also received training to participate in recruitment panels and to help facilitate training courses. In 2005, a group of children and young people was involved in making a film about their thoughts and feelings of being in foster care. This resource is now used in the training of staff and students on pre- and post-qualifying training courses.

You may already be aware of some creative youth group projects in your own community where various media, such as the internet, arts, drama or film have been used to voice the ideas of children and young people (Kirby et al., 2003a). There are many ways in which children and young people can express their views and experiences, and these different media can provide powerful illustrations of their lives, their problems and their strategies for change (Lansdown, 2001). However, whilst children themselves will have views and ideas on how to construct effective methods of involvement (Lansdown, 2001), a number of resources has been produced to help support you in enabling groups of children of all ages and abilities to participate in public decision-making processes. The Department for Education and Skills, for example, commissioned CRAE to develop a comprehensive set of training and tools to increase children and young people's effective participation in decision-making. The pack, which is called *Ready Steady Change* (CRAE, 2005), has been designed specifically to help practitioners ensure that children and young people's wishes, feelings and ideas are at the heart of future public decision-making, policy and service development. Another resource pack, the *Evaluator's Cookbook* (2005), which has been produced by the National Evaluation of the Children's Fund (NECF), contains 'recipes' for participatory evaluation exercises for use with children and young people. Interactive versions of some of these exercises are available on the NECF website, details of which appear at the end of this chapter. Whilst this is primarily a resource for professionals working with children aged 5–13 years, the exercises have been piloted for use with adults.

It is important to bear in mind that whilst children and young people are often not responsible for making the final decision in public decision-making processes, they can and do play an important role in informing and influencing an organisation's work (Kirby et al., 2003a). Moreover, children and young people, like adult service users and carers, can also play an important role in influencing the development of social policy. Arguably, in this context, social workers have a role to play in linking young service users and carers to wider campaign groups in society, so that their voices can be heard at a national level. In thinking back to Activity 6.5, you may have made a connection between the three levels of participation identified. Issues that start out as concerns for individual children and young people are often concerns that are shared by others. As we have seen, bringing children and young people together in groups enables them to engage in discussion with peers, and to work together to take action about their concerns. Where opportunities are provided for community-based groups to meet with other area groups, this can then provide a platform for children and young people's voices to be heard at a national level.

Participation in public decision-making at a national level tends to be dominated by involvement in formal activities, such as children and young people's contributions at conferences and presentations, campaign groups or the UK Youth Parliament. These opportunities to come together are important in enabling children and young people to make positive changes to policies and services, by empowering them through the strength of numbers. A National Voice, an organisation run by and for young people who have experience of being looked after in care, provides a national platform to hear the voices of young people from care. Working alongside the Department for Education and Skills, local authorities, youth organisations and other voluntary agencies, A National Voice consults with young people from care, and works to ensure that leading decision-makers are aware of, and act upon, young people's views (www.anationalvoice.org), as can be seen in the case study below.

> **CASE STUDY**
>
> 'This is NOT a Suitcase Campaign' was launched in 2003 by young people from A National Voice to put an end to the poor practice of moving children and young people between care placements with their possessions in black bin liners. The campaign has called for placing authorities to provide all children and young people with suitable luggage or a suitcase, and a request has been made that a 'no bin bag' policy is put in place. As part of this campaign, young people have staged catwalk protests at Tate Britain, one of which was entitled The 'Refuse Collection' Bin Bag Fashion Show, when young care leavers joined celebrities and other children's services representatives to model outfits made from black bin sacks. At the time of writing, more than 90 out of a possible 150 local authorities have signed up to the 'no bin bag charter'.
>
> (www.anationalvoice.org.uk)

As we saw in Chapter 2, government ministers demonstrated commitment to designing policies and services around the needs of children and young people through the Quality Protects Programme (DoH, 1998a). A recent example of this ongoing commitment is the guidance that was circulated to all local authorities clarifying the position in relation to overnight stays for children who are looked-after (DfES and DoH, 2004). Responding to concerns raised with government and the Children's Rights Director by many looked-after children, that normal social visits overnight were being impeded by local requirements for Criminal Records Bureau checks on adults at the households where they might stay overnight, the government set out guiding principles and good practice for making decisions about overnight stays. This guidance has made it easier for children and young people from care to stay at friends' houses overnight (DfES and DoH, 2004).

C H A P T E R   S U M M A R Y

This chapter has explored some of the different ways that you can encourage and facilitate the involvement and participation of children and young people in social work practice. We have examined some of the specific issues surrounding the participation of children and young people, and considered the implications of this for your own practice. In particular, opportunities have been provided for you to reflect on how your own attitudes about children and young people can influence the messages that you convey in your relations with them.

We have also explored some of the challenges of supporting and sustaining participation, and have identified some of the key skills that you will need to develop in order to facilitate effectively children and young people's involvement in collective and individual decision-making processes. Throughout the chapter, we have argued that approaches to the involvement of children and young people need to be engaging, creative and child-centred. A participation triangle (Figure 6.3) is used in the final part of the chapter, to examine some of the methods and approaches that you can use across the three different levels of participation. A number of guides and resource packs on facilitating children and young people's participation has been recommended. These resources will be helpful in providing you with a plethora of creative activities to listen to children and young people, and to help them voice their feelings, views and opinions.

Children's Rights Alliance for England (CRAE) (2005) *Ready steady change participation training materials*. London: CRAE.

A useful set of training and resource materials for practitioners, children and young people concerned with empowering children as decision-makers.

Hutton, A and Partridge, K (2006) *Say it your own way: Children's participation in assessment*. Barkingside: Barnado's; Department for Education and Skills.

A practical resource guide to support professionals in facilitating children's participation in assessment processes.

Lansdown, G (2001) *Promoting children's participation in democratic decision-making*. Florence: UNICEF Innocenti Research Centre (Innocenti Insight, A 6).

This useful publication provides practical guidance on the lessons to be learned to date about working with children and young people as partners. It makes a positive contribution to the development of tools for those who are committed to ensuring that the rights of children are heard.

National Evaluation of the Children's Fund (NECF) (2005) *The Evaluator's Cookbook. Participatory evaluation exercises. A resource book for work with children and young people*. **www.ne-cf.org**

A clear and easily accessible resource containing ideas for participatory evaluation exercises developed by NECF staff, Children's Fund workers drawing, in particular, on the work of Katrice Horsley, Katalysttales.

Shephard, C and Treseder, P (2002) *Participation – spice it up!: Practical tools for engaging children and young people in planning and consultations*. Cardiff: Save the Children.

A user-friendly practical resource that provides a range of easy-to-follow participation activities. Includes useful ideas about how to creatively adapt the activities presented.

Wright, P, Turner, C, Clay, D and Mills, H (2006) *The participation of children and young people in developing social care*. Practice participation guide 6. London: Social Care Institute for Excellence.

This practice guide explores how social care staff can initiate and sustain the participation of children and young people in service development.

www.anationalvoice.org A National Voice

This is the website for A National Voice, the only organisation in England run by and for young people from care to enable these young people to speak out on issues that affect their lives.

www.avoice4us.com AVoice4 us

This is a website for looked-after children in Cambridgeshire. It aims to find out what children and young people think about their services, and to get them to become more interested and involved in their care. It also provides information about the services and advice that are available, such as the locally based 'Just Us' groups.

www.participationworks.org.uk Participation Works

This website provides access to some of the latest thinking and research about children and young people's participation. In addition to the knowledge hub, it provides connections with networks of practitioners and access to training resources for children, young people and adults.

Conclusion

This book has taken a distinctive look at social work practice within the specific practice context of service user and carer involvement and participation. As you have seen, the importance of involving service users and carers has been a central theme of the government's modernisation agenda in health and social care developments. This need for service user and carer participation stems from a desire to raise standards in service delivery so that services are improved and become more effective in meeting diverse needs. As a consequence, agencies are now required to engage service users and carers in their assessments, in service management, planning, quality assurance, training and research.

Throughout this book, you have been encouraged to explore a perspective on working with service users and carers that values the richness and diversity of their knowledge and experience. Emphasis has been placed on the need to recognise service users and carers as experts in their own lives, and to empower them to take and maintain control over the decision-making processes that affect their lives. All of this demands a high level of interpersonal skill and a clarity of communication so that you are able to get alongside people, listen to them and respond effectively. The knowledge, skills and values that you develop during your training will help you to be effective in making a difference to the lives of those service users and carers with whom you work. This text, along with others in the series, will contribute to this development.

Service user and carer involvement and participation in social work practice is both challenging and rewarding. In each situation in which you are working with a service user or carer you will need to take account of the whole range of issues covered in this book. We hope that as you have studied this book, you have been encouraged to reflect upon your developing knowledge, and that you will take your studies further by exploring the recommended reading and internet sources that have been suggested at the end of each chapter. You may find it helpful to spend some time reflecting on the key themes of this book, your own learning with regard to service user and carer participation, and how you might meet the six National Occupational Standards for social work and promote the values enshrined in the Code of Practice for social workers.

This book can be used in ways that allow you to revisit aspects of service user and carer participation. If there are elements that you have found difficult or need to enhance, for example, you can return to individual chapters or single activities at any time. We hope that the learning that you have gained from this text will contribute to your development as a professional social worker by enabling you to work more effectively in partnership with service users and carers. You will, of course, need to build on this learning by continuing to develop your practice, and by updating your knowledge and skills. The way in which you develop your learning further will be, to some extent, unique to you.

Appendix

Timeline of the development of service users' and carers' movements

Developments in legislation and policy

International developments

Timeline	Development of the Adult Carers' Movement	Development of the Mental Health System Survivors' Movement	Development of the Disabled People's Movement
1960s			
1964			France: Group for Independence of Physically Disabled Persons formed.
1965	National Council for the Single Woman and Her Dependants formed (NCSWD). Campaigned for financial support for carers.		Disablement Income Group (DIG) formed to campaign for a comprehensive disability income.
1967	Dependent relative tax allowance increased. Women needing to give up work to care granted pension credits.		
1969		PNP – People Need People (People Not Psychiatry) formed.	
1970s		PNP network developed; The National Schizophrenia Society founded.	Berkeley, California: Independent Living Movement began.
		Chronically Sick and Disabled Persons Act 1970: Local authority duty to assess general needs and numbers, and provide a range of practical services.	
1971		National Association for Mental Health (NAMH) launched a public education and fund-raising campaign, changing its emphasis to a lobbying group.	National rally to campaign for improvements to mobility provision. Formation of The Association of Disabled Professionals (ADP).
	Attendance Allowance introduced for people needing constant care at home.		
1972		National Association for Mental Health (NAMH) renamed Mind; Schizophrenia Fellowship registered as a charity.	
1973		Mental Patients' Union formed to challenge repressive psychiatric practice, and to support and secure rights of representation for mental health patients.	USA: The Rehabilitation Act prohibited discrimination.
1974		Schizophrenia Fellowship renamed The National Schizophrenia Fellowship (NSF).	Formation of the Disability Alliance (DA) to reduce poverty among disabled people; The Union of Physically Impaired Against Segregation (UPIAS) formed by disabled people.

Timeline	Development of the Adult Carers' Movement	Development of the Mental Health System Survivors' Movement	Development of the Disabled People's Movement
			Spinal Injuries Association (SIA) established – one of the first charities managed by service users.
			Appointment of the First Minister for the Disabled.
			American Coalition of Citizens with Disabilities (ACCD) formed.
1975			Discussion about the differences between the Union of Physically Impaired Against Segregation (UPIAS) and the Disability Alliance, led to UPIAS building a new organisation to campaign for the inclusion of disabled people into mainstream society.
		White Paper *Better Services for the Mentally Ill* (HM Government, 1975): set out the government's strategy for future service development, proposing local-based care.	United Nations Declaration of the Rights of Disabled Persons.
1976	Invalid Care Allowance introduced – first benefit specifically for carers.	Mind's 'Home from Hospital' campaign highlighted the housing problems experienced by people with mental illness; pressure group Protection of the Rights of Mental Patients in Therapy (PROMPT) established to protect the rights of mental health patients.	National Union of the Deaf formed; the Union of Physically Impaired Against Segregation (UPIAS) published *Fundamental Principles of Disability* which promoted a new way of thinking about disability as social oppression (the social model).
			Chronically Sick and Disabled Persons (Amendment) Act 1976: extended provision of CSDP Act 1970 and provided for access to employment premises.
1977	USA: Family Caregiver Alliance founded, beginning the national movement.		Royal Association of Disability and Rehabilitation formed (RADAR)
1978	Home Responsibilities Protection introduced to protect carers' basic state pension.		
1979			Committee on Restrictions against Disabled People (CORAD) set up to examine the structural and institutional context of discrimination.
1980s	Australia: Carers Association of New South Wales founded.		
1981	The National Council changed its name to The National Council for Carers and their Elderly Dependants (NCCED) to reflect demographic changes; Association of Carers formed – first organisation for all carers, regardless of sex or age.		First Coalition of Disabled People formed – a campaigning organisation controlled by disabled people. National umbrella organisation, the British Council of Organisations of Disabled People (BCODP) formed to promote the full equality and participation of all disabled people in society; 'See Hear' TV series started.
			Disabled Persons Act 1981: dealt with issues of access and adaptations to buildings to cater for workers with mobility problems.
			International Year of Disabled People; Disabled Peoples' International (DPI) formed – first World Congress held.

Timeline	Development of the Adult Carers' Movement	Development of the Mental Health System Survivors' Movement	Development of the Disabled People's Movement
1982			Committee on Restrictions against Disabled People recommended the introduction of anti-discrimination legislation.
			Adoption of the United Nations World Programme of action concerning disabled people.
1983		Mental Health Act 1983: aimed to safeguard people's rights and protect their interests during and following compulsory admission to hospital.	UN proclaimed a Decade of Disabled Persons (1983–1992) to implement the World Programme of Action; National campaign by American Disabled for Accessible Public Transit (ADAPT).
1984			Formation of Disabled People South Africa, a national umbrella organisation; UN Declaration of Human Rights amended to include disabled people's rights.
1985	Association of Carers campaigned to extend Invalid Care Allowance to married and cohabiting women.	Companies Act 1985: required large companies to publish policy on how they recruited, trained and promoted disabled members of staff.	
		USA: National Association of Psychiatric Survivors founded; First World Mental Health Conference held in Brighton: The Mind/World Federation for Mental Health Congress.	Voluntary Organisations for Anti-Discrimination Legislation (VOADL) set up.
1986	The National Council for Carers and their Elderly Dependants (NCCED) and the Association of Carers began to work together to create one voice for carers to government, political parties and the media.	Campaign Against Psychiatric Oppression (CAPO) formed out of PROMPT. The first national network of survivors mental health services, Survivors Speak Out (SSO), established to support the formation of independent service user groups; National Voices Forum established, a service-oriented user network within the National Schizophrenia Fellowship; awareness raised by service users produced national TV programme 'We're not Mad ... We're Angry'.	Formation of the regional partnership, South African Federation of Disabled People (SAFOD).
	European Court of Justice ruling prompts government to extend Invalid Care Allowance to married and co-habiting carers.		
	Disabled Persons (Services, Consultation and Representation) Act 1986: Local authorities required to publish relevant services, to involve people with disabilities in decisions and to take into account a carer's ability to care.		
1987		Mind Link was established as a forum for service users to influence the policy of Mind.	
1988	The National Council for Carers and their Elderly Dependants (NCCED) and the Association of Carers merged to form the Carers National Association.	National telephone helpline for women launched by Bristol Crisis Service for Women (BCSW). Formation of first UK Hearing Voices group.	'Rights not Charity' march in London; Independent Living Fund established.
	Griffiths Report: recognition that carers are the main providers of community care.		Canada: first National Access Awareness week; National disability umbrella organisation, All-Russian Society of Disabled People (ARSD), formed.
1989	White Paper *Caring for people: Community care in the next decade and beyond* (DoH, 1989) recognised that the majority of community care is provided by carers.	First national conference on self-harm organised by the user movement.	Children Act 1989: provided some rights to disabled children.

Timeline	Development of the Adult Carers' Movement	Development of the Mental Health System Survivors' Movement	Development of the Disabled People's Movement
	An alliance of voluntary organisations and Carers National Association secured an amendment to the NHS and Community Care Bill, making it a duty for local authorities to consult with carers when drawing up community care plans. They were unsuccessful in securing a right to an assessment for carers.		
	Australia: Carers Queensland and Carers Association of South Australia founded.		
1990s	National Health Service and Community Care Act 1990: Local authority duty to assess an individual's needs for community care services; to consult with stakeholders regarding the publication of plans for community care services and to recognise people who provide care as 'carers'. Policy guidance accompanying the Act was the first government document to discuss carers' involvement in service users' assessments.		
	Carers National Association continued to campaign for the rights of carers to a separate assessment.	Umbrella organisation UK Advocacy Network (UKAN) founded to promote the development of advocacy groups and service user involvement projects. Hearing Voices Network set up self-help groups to provide information and support and to challenge medical approaches.	National demonstrations demanding full citizenship rights and a proper income for disabled people; demonstrations at London Weekend Television Studios against 'Telethon'.
			USA: The Americans with Disabilities Act extended the provision of the Rehabilitation Act.
1991	The Princess Royal Trust for Carers formed.		BCODP launched its campaign for anti-discrimination legislation.
	Getting it Right for Carers (DoH and SSI, 1991b) first policy guidance on how to approach assessing carers' needs locally.		
1992		International disability and human rights network, Disability Awareness in Action (DAA), formed to support self-advocacy, provide an information exchange network and promote and protect people's human rights world-wide.	
			Second 'Block Telethon' demonstration. 'Rights Now!' group, an extension of the VOADL, formed to organise and co-ordinate events around campaigning, promoting and publicising the need for anti-discrimination legislation.
1993	Carers National Association lobbied MPs to take on a Private Members Bill.	Documents on service user charters, training and education, and advocacy code of practice produced by the Mental Health Task Force User Group (1992–4).	Disabled Persons Direct Action Network (DAN) formed to campaign for changes through direct action.
	Carers Association of Australia and National Family Caregivers Association, USA founded.		
1994		*Finding a Place: A Review of Mental Health Services for Adults* (Audit Commission, 1994) identified deficiencies in existing service provision and proposed improvements.	Spastic Society renamed Scope.

Timeline	Development of the Adult Carers' Movement	Development of the Mental Health System Survivors' Movement	Development of the Disabled People's Movement
		Mind 'Breakthrough! Community Care' campaign promoted a service user-centred holistic approach to community care. Mind Yellow Card Scheme set up providing opportunities for users to report on the side-effects of their drugs. User-led National Self-Harm Network (NSHN) established to provide support to, and campaign for the rights of people who self-harm.	Malaysia: Demonstration by disabled people demanding an accessible monorail in Kuala Lumpur.
		Government used procedural means to defeat the Civil Rights (Disabled Persons) Bill, causing public outrage.	
1995	The Carers (Recognition and Services) Act 1995 gave carers a right to an assessment of their ability to provide, and to continue to provide care.	Mental Health (Patients in the Community) Act 1995: provided powers for the supervised discharge of some patients following compulsory detention.	'Rights Now!' campaign for civil rights legislation. British Council of Organisations of Disabled People renamed British Council of Disabled People.
			Russia: adopted the Law on Social Protection of Disabled People.
		Disability Discrimination Act 1995: gave disabled people rights with regard to employment, the provision of goods, facilities and services, the disposal or management of premises, education and public transport. Caused outrage within the disability movement.	
1996	Carers National Association campaigned for more breaks, better funding for services, increased benefits and higher quality services for carers.	Community Care (Direct Payments) Act 1996: empowered local authorities to provide cash payments for some people assessed as needing community care services, to enable them to organise their own arrangements for services.	
	USA: Foundation of the National Alliance for Caregiving, a coalition of national organisations focusing on issues of family care.		
1997		Mind's 'Respect' campaign highlighted the discrimination experienced by people with mental illness. Diverse Minds initiative set up to ensure Mind's policy and practice was more responsive to black and minority ethnic communities. Self-management pioneered by the Manic Depression Fellowship.	
		Disability Rights Task Force set up to advise the government on the action required to promote comprehensive and enforceable civil rights for disabled people.	
1998	*Modernising Mental Health Services – Safe, Sound and Supportive* (DoH, 1998b): set out a vision for mental health services for adults and acknowledged the need to involve patients, service users and carers in their own care, and in planning services.		
	Quality Protects Initiative (DoH, 1998a): A key objective was to ensure that children whose parents had specific needs arising out of disability or health conditions (relevant to young carers) enjoyed the same life chances as all other children in the locality.	The Mental After Care Association for Poor Persons Convalescent or Recovered from Institutions for the Insane renamed Maca (The Mental After Care Association) – widened the scope of its work to include research, education and campaigning.	
	'Caring for Carers', first International Conference on Family Care, London.		

Timeline	Development of the Adult Carers' Movement	Development of the Mental Health System Survivors' Movement	Development of the Disabled People's Movement
	The Human Rights Act 1998: enshrined European Convention on Human Rights into UK law.		
1999	*National Strategy for Carers* (DoH, 1999a) launched to improve the situation and support for all carers; Employment Relations Act 1999 marked the first right for working carers to time off work for emergencies.	Formation of the Mental Health Alliance, a coalition of organisations established to improve mental health legislation. Mad Pride, with its emphasis on the celebration of 'mad culture' and involvement in direct action, formed.	'Free Our People' campaign launched by Disabled Persons' Direct Action Network.
	National Service Framework for Mental Health (DoH, 1999d) established national standards for promoting mental health and carers' assessments.		
	Disability Rights Commission Act 1999: set up a body to work towards eliminating discrimination, to promote equal opportunities, to encourage good practice in the treatment of disabled people and to keep under review the working of the Disability Discrimination Act 1995.		
2000s	Carers National Association launched the 'Fair Deal' Campaign to highlight the financial implications of caring.		Disability Rights Commission launched.
	Carers and Disabled Children Act 2000: gave carers over the age of 16 years new rights to services in their own right, an assessment of their needs independent of the person needing care, direct payments and vouchers for short-term breaks.	Mental Health Alliance lobbied Parliament to press for changes to the government's plans to reform the Mental Health Act.	
	Child Support, Pensions and Social Security Act 2000: introduced the State Second Pension, allowing carers to build a second tier state pension.		
	Carers recognised as key partners in the NHS National Plan (ten-year plan).		
2001	Carers UK launched 'Carers' Health Matters' campaign focusing on the recognition of carers' health needs and the need for carers' views to shape service delivery in the NHS; Carers National Association renamed Carers UK. New campaign launched to improve the recognition of carers.		
2002	Carers UK's campaign on work-related issues.	The National Schizophrenia Fellowship renamed Rethink; proposed new Mental Health Act opposed by newly-formed campaign group 'No Force'; national demonstrations against draft Mental Health Bill.	DAN and BCODP drafted the Disabled People Rights and Freedoms Bill to replace the Disability Discrimination Act 1995.
	The Employment Act: gave parents of disabled children the right to request flexible working arrangements from their employer. Working Family Tax credit with higher levels of benefits for parents of disabled children introduced; carers over 65 became entitled to Carers Allowance.		

Timeline	Development of the Adult Carers' Movement	Development of the Mental Health System Survivors' Movement	Development of the Disabled People's Movement
2003	The Community Care (Delayed Discharges) Act: gave carers new rights to services before a patient is discharged from hospital.		Campaigners lobbied Parliament to win support for the draft Disabled People's Rights and Freedoms Bill; UK Disabled People's Parliament launched – debated civil rights law for disabled people.
			European Year of Disabled People.
	Patient and Public Involvement Forums (PPI) set up to enable patients, carers and members of the public to influence the organisation and delivery of local health services.		
2004	International Alliance of Carers Organisations (IACO) launched by family care-giving organisations from Australia, Sweden, the Netherlands, UK and USA.		Draft Disabled People's Rights and Freedoms Bill put forward as an alternative to the government's draft Disability Discrimination Bill.
2005	Carers (Equal Opportunities) Act 2005: gave carers new rights to information and ensured that all carers' assessments consider their leisure, education, training and work.		
	Launch of Carers UK 'Back me up' campaign to ensure the availability of emergency replacement care services, and 'Make WORK Work' campaign to give carers real choices about balancing work with caring.	Disability Discrimination Act 2005: amended or extended existing provision with regard to the definition of disability; access to and use of premises, private clubs and transport; public sector duties to promote equality of opportunity for disabled people.	
		The Mental After Care Association (Maca) changed its name to 'Together: Working for Wellbeing' to reflect the changes in emphasis of its work.	
2006	Work and Families Act 2006: extended to carers of adults, the right to request flexible working; White Paper *Our health, our care, our say* (DoH, 2006a): set out a vision to provide people with good quality community services. Promised more support for carers including improved home-based emergency respite services and the establishment of a national helpline. Also provided for the extension of direct payments to service users and the piloting of individual budgets for social care.		
		Government abandoned controversial draft Mental Health Bill. New shorter bill to amend existing Mental Health Act 1983 proposed.	British Council of Disabled People renamed UK Disabled People's Council.

Sources: Campbell, 1996, 2006; Evans, 1996; Barnes, 1998, 2000; Carers UK, 2002, 2005, 2007; Rethink, 2002; Aldridge and Becker, 2003; Darton, 2006; DRTF, 2006; Millington, 2006; Roberts, 2006; Stewart, 2006; Together Working for Wellbeing, 2006; UK Disabled People's Council, 2006; Disability Awareness in Action, 2007; UKAN, 2007.

References

Adams, R (2003) *Social work and empowerment.* 3rd edition. Basingstoke: Palgrave Macmillan.

Adcock, M (2001) The core assessment process. How to synthesise information and make judgements, in Howarth, J (ed.) *The child's world. Assessing children in need.* London: Jessica Kingsley Publishers.

Age Concern (2005) *How ageist is Britain?* **www.ageconcern.co.uk/AgeConcern/Documents/how_ageist_is_britain(1).pdf**

Alderson, P (1993) *Children's consent to surgery.* Buckingham: Open University Press.

Aldgate, J and Statham, J (2001) *The Children Act now. Messages from research.* London: Stationery Office.

Aldridge, J and Becker, S (1993) *Children who care. Inside the world of young carers.* Loughborough: Young Carers Research Group, Department of Social Sciences, Loughborough University.

Aldridge, J and Becker, S (2003) *Children caring for parents with mental illness. Perspectives of young carers, parents and professionals.* Bristol: The Policy Press.

Allan, K (2001) *Communication and consultation: exploring ways for staff to involve people with dementia in developing services.* Bristol: The Policy Press.

Arksey, H, Jackson, K, Wallace, A, Baldwin, S, Golder, S, Newbronner, E and Hare, P (2003) *Access to health care for carers: Barriers and interventions. Report for the National   Co-ordinating Centre for NHS Service Delivery and Organisation Research and Development (NCCSDO).* **www.sdo.lshtm.ac.uk/files/project/24-final-report.pdf**

Audit Commission (1992) *Community care: Managing the cascade of change.* London: HMSO.

Audit Commission (1994) *Finding a place: A review of mental health services for adults.* London: HMSO.

Audit Commission and Social Services Inspectorate (SSI) (2002) *Joint reviews undertaken in 2002.* **www.audit-commission.gov.uk/reports/product_list.asp?prodType=JOINT-REVIEW**

Audit Commission and Social Services Inspectorate (SSI) (2003) *Joint Reviews undertaken in 2003.* **www.audit-commission.gov.uk/reports/product_list.asp?prodType=JOINT-REVIEW**

Audit Commission and Social Services Inspectorate (SSI) (2004) *Joint Reviews undertaken in 2004.* **www.audit-commission.gov.uk/reports/product_list.asp?prodType=JOINT-REVIEW**

Bannister, A (2001) Entering the child's world. Communicating with children to assess their needs, in Howarth, J (ed.) *The child's world. Assessing children in need.* London: Jessica Kingsley Publishers.

Barnes, C (1998) The social model of disability: A sociological phenomenon ignored by sociologists?, in Shakespeare, T (ed.) *The disability reader: Social science perspectives.* London: Cassell.

Barnes, C (2000) *Disabled people in Britain and discrimination. A case for anti-discrimination legislation.* London: Hurst and Company.

Barnes, J (2002) *Reform of social work education and training. Focus on the future. Key messages from focus groups about the future of social work training.* **www.dh.gov.uk/assetRoot/04/08/23/ 78/04082378.pdf**

Barnes, C, Morgan, H and Mercer, G (2001) *Creating independent futures: an evaluation of services led by disabled people. Stage three report.* **www.leeds.ac.uk/disability-studies/archiveuk/Barnes/S3 Report.pdf**

Barnes, C, Mercer, G with Din, I (2003) *Research review on user involvement in promoting change and enhancing the quality of social 'care' services for disabled people.* **www.leeds.ac.uk/disability-studies/archiveuk/archframe.htm**

Becker, S (2000) Young carers, in Davies, M (ed.) *The Blackwell encyclopaedia of social work.* Oxford: Blackwell.

Becker, S, Aldridge, J and Dearden, C (1998) *Young carers and their families.* Oxford: Blackwell Science.

Begum, N (2006) *Doing it for themselves: participation and black and minority ethnic service users.* Participation report 14. **www.scie.org.uk/publications/reports/report14.pdf**

Beresford, P (1994) *Changing the culture: involving service users in social work education.* Paper 32.4. London: Central Council for Education and Training in Social Work.

Beresford, P (2000) Service users' knowledges and social work theory: conflict or collaboration. *British Journal of Social Work*, 30 (4), 489–503.

Beresford, P and Campbell, J (1994) Disabled people, service users, user involvement and representation. *Disability and Society*, 9 (3), 315–325.

Beresford, P and Croft, S (1993) *Citizen involvement: a practical guide for change.* London: Macmillan.

Beresford, P and Croft, S (2004) Service users and practitioners reunited: the key component for social work reform. *British Journal of Social Work*, 34 (1), 53–68.

Beresford, P, Shamash, M, Forrest, V, Turner, M and Branfield, F (2005) *Developing social care: service users' vision for adult support.* Report 7. **www.scie.org.uk/publications/ reports/report07.pdf**

Brandon, M, Schofield, G and Trinder, L (1998) *Social work with children.* Basingstoke: Palgrave.

Braye, S (2000) Participation and involvement in social care. An overview, in Kemshall, H and Littlechild, R (eds) *User involvement and participation in social care. Research Informing Practice.* London: Jessica Kingsley Publishers.

British Council of Disabled People (2006) *Welcome to the British Council of Disabled People.* **www.bcodp.org.uk**

British Deaf Association (1996) *Deaf people's participation in local services.* Joseph Rowntree Foundation Findings. **www.jrf.org.uk/knowledge/findings/socialcare/ SC77.asp**

Butler, I and Roberts, G (1997) *Social work with children and families. Getting into practice.* London: Jessica Kingsley Publishers.

Butt, J and O'Neil, A (2004) *'Let's move on': Black and minority ethnic older people's views on research findings.* York: Joseph Rowntree Foundation.

Cairney, J, Chettle, K, Clark, M, Davis, A, Gosling, J, Harvey, R, Jephcote, S, Labana, L, Lymbery, M, Pendred, B and Russell, L (2006) Editorial. *Social Work Education*, 25 (4), 315–318.

Cameron, L and Murphy, J (2002) Enabling young people with a learning disability to make choices at a time of transition. *British Journal of Learning Disabilities*, 30 (3), 105–112.

Campbell, P (1996) The history of the user movement in the United Kingdom, in Heller, T, Reynolds, J, Gomm, R, Muston, R, and Pattison, S (eds) *Mental health matters: A reader.* London: Macmillan Press.

Campbell, P (2005) From little acorns. The mental health service user movement, in Bell, A and Lindley, P (eds) *Beyond the water towers. The unfinished revolution in mental health services 1985–2005.* London: The Sainsbury Centre for Mental Health.

Campbell, P (2006) *Some things you should know about user/survivor action: a Mind resource pack.* London: Mind.

Care Council for Wales (2002) *Code of practice for social care workers and code of practice for employers of social care workers.* Cardiff: Care Council for Wales.

Carers UK (2002) *The history of Carers UK and the carers movement.* **www.carersuk.org.uk**

Carers UK (2005) *Strategic plan 2005-2008.* **www.carersuk.org.uk**

Carers UK (2007) *Carers UK success and achievements.* **www.carersuk.org.uk**

Carnaby, S (1997) 'What do you think?': a qualitative approach to evaluating individual planning services. *Journal of Intellectual Disability Research*, 41 (3), 225–231.

Carpenter, J and Sbaraini, S (1997) *Choice, information and dignity involving users and carers in care management in mental health.* Bristol: The Policy Press.

Carr, S (2004) *Has service user participation made a difference to social care services?* Position paper 3. **www.scie.org.uk/publications/positionpapers/pp03.pdf**

Carter, T and Beresford, P (2000) *Age and change: models of involvement for older people.* York: York Publishing Services.

Chahal, K and Ullah, AI (2004) *Experiencing ethnicity: discrimination and service provision.* Foundations. **www.jrf.org.uk/knowledge/findings/foundations/914.asp**

Children and Young People's Unit (CYPU) (2001) *Learning to listen – Core principles for the involvement of children and young people.* London: Department for Education   and Employment.

Children Now (2006) *The participation charter.* **www.childrennow.co.uk/charter**

Children's Rights Alliance for England (CRAE) (2005) *Ready steady change participation training materials.* London: CRAE.

Children's Rights Officers and Advocates (CROA) (2000) *Total respect handbook.* London: Children's Rights Officers and Advocates and Department of Health.

Children's Society (2006) *Young people's key skill development training manual.* **www.childrens society.org.uk/NR/rdonlyres/BDD2FE73-B5A1-4029-80B2-FA7264444 584/0/LetMEBeHeard.pdf**

Citizens as Trainers and Young Independent People Presenting Educational Entertainment (CATS and YIPPEE) (2002) Skills and knowledge needed by social workers, in CATS and YIPPEE *How to involve service users.* Salford: YIPPEE and CATS, University of Salford.

Citizens as Trainers (CATS), Young Independent People Presenting Educational Entertainment (YIPPEE), Rimmer, A and Harwood, K (2004) Citizen participation in the education and training of social workers. *Social Work Education*, 23 (3), 309–323.

Clare, L and Cox, S (2003) Improving service approaches and outcomes for people with complex needs through consultation and involvement. *Disability and Society*, 18 (7), 935–953.

Community Care Needs Assessment Project (CCNAP) (2001) 'Asking the Experts'. *A guide to involving people in shaping health and social care services*. **www.ccnap.org.uk/ InvolvingPeople/theguide.htm**

Convention of Scottish Local Authorities (COSLA) (2002) *Focusing on citizens: A guide to approaches and methods*. **www.dundeecity.gov.uk/ce**

Cordingley, L, Hughes, J and Challis, D (2001) *Unmet need and older people: Towards a synthesis of user and provider views*. York: Joseph Rowntree Foundation.

Crawford, K and Walker, J (2003) *Social work and human development*. Exeter: Learning Matters.

Crawford, M, Rutter, D and Thelwall, S (2003) *User involvement in change management: A review of the literature. Report to the National Co-ordinating Centre for NHS Service Delivery and Organisation Research and Development (NCCSDO)*. **www.sdo.lshtm. ac.uk/files/project/18-final-report.pdf**

Croft, S and Beresford, P (1996) The politics of participation, in Taylor, DL (ed.) *Critical social policy: A reader*. London: Sage Publications.

Cutler, D (2003) *Standard! Organisational standards and young people's participation in public decision making*. London: Carnegie Young People Initiative. **www.carnegieuktrust.org.uk/files/main/ Standard%20Report.pdf**

Cutler, D and Taylor, A (2003) *Expanding and sustaining involvement. A snapshot of participation infrastructure for young people living in England*. London: Carnegie Young People Initiative. **www.dfes.gov.uk/research/data/uploadfiles/Expandingandsustaining.pdf**

Dalyrymple, J and Burke, B (1999) *Anti-oppressive practice. Social care and the law*. Buckingham: Open University Press.

Danso, C, Greaves, H, Howell, S, Ryan, M, Sinclair, R and Tunnard, J (2003) *The involvement of children and young people in promoting change and enhancing the quality of services: A research report for SCIE from the National Children's Bureau*. London: National Children's Bureau.

Darton, K (2006) *History of Mind, the National Association of Mental Health, Mind Information Unit factsheet*. **www.mind.org.uk/Information/Factsheets/History+of+mental+health/History+of+Mind+ +The+National+Association+for+Mental+Health.htm**

Department for Education and Skills (DfES) (2003) *Every child matters*. London: The Stationery Office.

Department for Education and Skills and Department of Health (DfES and DoH) (2004) *Guidance on the delegation of decisions on 'overnight stays' for looked after children, LAC (2004) 4*. **www.dh.gov.uk/assetRoot/04/07/43/11/04074311.PDF**

Department of Health (1989) *Caring for people: Community care in the next decade and beyond*. London: HMSO.

Department of Health (DoH) (1990) *Community care in the next decade and beyond: Policy guidance*. London: HMSO.

Department of Health (DoH) (1994) *Community care: Framework for local community care charters in England*. London: Department of Health.

Department of Health (DoH) (1996a) *Consultation counts: Guidelines for service purchasers and users and carers based on the experiences of the national user and carer group*. London: Department of Health.

Department of Health (DoH) (1996b) *Children's services planning guidance LAC (96) 10*. London: Department of Health.

Department of Health (DoH) (1998a) *Quality protects: Framework for action*. London: HMSO.

Department of Health (DoH) (1998b) *Modernising mental health services: Safe, sound and supportive*. London: The Stationery Office.

Department of Health (DoH) (1998c) *Modernising social services: Promoting independence, improving protection, raising standards*. London: The Stationery Office.

Department of Health (DoH) (1999a) *Caring about carers – A national strategy for carers*. London: Department of Health.

Department of Health (DoH) (1999b) *UK national standards for foster care*. London: Department of Health.

Department of Health (DoH) (1999c) *The government's objectives for children's social services. Summary*. London: Department of Health.

Department of Health (DoH) (1999d) *National service framework for mental health. Modern standards and service models*. London: Department of Health.

Department of Health (DoH) (1999e) *Better care, higher standards. A charter for long term care*. London: Department of Health.

Department of Health (DoH) (2000a) *Framework for the assessment of children in need and their families*. London: Department of Health.

Department of Health (DoH) (2000b) *A quality strategy for social care*. London: Department of Health.

Department of Health (DoH) (2001a) *Valuing people: A new strategy for learning disability for the twenty-first century*. London: The Stationery Office.

Department of Health (DoH) (2001b) *National service framework for older people*. London: Department of Health.

Department of Health (DoH) (2002a) *The single assessment process guidance for local implementation. Annexes*. **www.dh.gov.uk/assetRoot/04/08/63/62/04086362.pdf**

Department of Health (DoH) (2002b) *Requirements for social work training*. London: Department of Health.

Department of Health (DoH) (2002c) *Listening, hearing and responding. Department of Health action plan: Core principles for the involvement of children and young people*. London: Department of Health.

Department of Health (DoH) (2002d) *National standards for the provision of children's advocacy services*. London: Department of Health.

Department of Health (DoH) (2003) *Strengthening accountability. Involving patients and the public. Practice guidance. Section 11 of the Health and Social Care Act 2004*. London: Department of Health.

Department of Health (DoH) (2004) *National service framework for children, young people and maternity services*. London: Department of Health.

Department of Health (DoH) (2006a) *Our health, our care, our say: a new direction for community services*. London: Department of Health.

Department of Health (DoH) (2006b) *Reward and recognition: the principles and practice of service user payment and reimbursement in health and social care. A guide for service providers, service users and carers.* 2nd edn. London: Department of Health.

Department of Health, Home Office and Department for Education and Employment (DoH, HO and DfEE) (1999) *Working together to safeguard children: A guide to inter-agency working to safeguard and promote the welfare of children.* London: Department of Health.

Department of Health and Social Services Inspectorate (DoH and SSI) (1991a) *Care management and assessment: Summary of practice guidance.* London: HMSO.

Department of Health and Social Services Inspectorate (DoH and SSI) (1991b) *Getting it right for carers: A guide for practitioners.* London: HMSO.

Department of Health and Social Services Inspectorate (DoH and SSI) (1997) *When leaving home is also leaving care. An inspection of services for young people leaving care.* London: Department of Health.

Disability Awareness in Action (2007) *About DAA.* **www.daa.org.uk**

Disability Rights Task Force (DRTF) (2006) *From inclusion to exclusion.* **www.dft.gov.uk**

Dybwad, G and Bersani, H (eds) (1996) *New voices: Self-advocacy by people with disabilities.* Cambridge, Massachusetts: Brookline Books.

Evans, J (1996) *Campaign for Civil Rights Legislation.* **www.independentliving.org**

Evans, R and Banton, M (2001) *Involving black disabled people in shaping services,* Joseph Rowntree Foundation Findings. **www.jrf.org.uk/knowledge/findings/socialcare/d61.asp**

Evans, C and Fisher, M (1999) Collaborative evaluation with service users. Moving towards user-controlled research, in Shaw, I and Lishman, J (eds) *Evaluation and social work practice.* London: Sage Publications.

Faulkner, A and Layzell, S (2000) *Strategies for living: A report of user-led research into people's strategies for living with mental distress.* London: Mental Health Foundation.

Finlay, WML and Lyons, E (2002) Acquiescence in interviews with people who have mental retardation. *Mental Retardation,* 40, 14–29.

Frank, J (2002) *Making it work. Good practice with young carers and their families.* London: The Children's Society and The Princess Royal Trust for Carers.

Franklin, A and Sloper, P (2004) Participation of disabled children and young people in decision-making within social services departments. A survey of current and recent activities in social services in England. **www.york.ac.uk/inst/spru/research/pdf/quality protects.pdf**

General Social Care Council (GSCC) (2002) *Code of practice for social care workers and code of practice for employers of social care workers.* London: General Social Care Council.

Hafford-Letchfield, T (2006) *Management and organisations in social work.* Exeter: Learning Matters.

Hart, RA (1997) *Children's participation: The theory and practice of involving young citizens in community development and environmental care.* London: Earthscan.

Heffernan, K (2006) Social work, new public management and the language of 'service user'. *British Journal of Social Work,* 36 (1), 139–147.

Heron, C (1998) *Working with carers*. London: Jessica Kingsley Publishers.

Higham, P (2005) *What is important about social work and social care?* **www.ssrg.org.uk/ assembly/files/patriciahigham.pdf**

HM Government (1975) *Better services for the mentally ill*. London: HMSO.

HM Government (2006) *Working together to safeguard children: A guide to inter-agency working to safeguard and promote the welfare of children*. London: The Stationery Office.

Howe, D (1992) Theories of helping, empowerment and participation, in Thoburn, J (ed.) *Participation in practice – involving families in child protection: A reader*. Norwich: UEA/Department of Health.

Hutton, A and Partridge, K (2006) *Say it your own way: children's participation in assessment*. Barkingside: Barnado's; Department for Education and Skills.

Janzon, K and Law, S (2003) *Older people influencing social care: aspirations and realities. Research review on user involvement in promoting change and enhancing the quality of social care services*. Care Equation Ltd.

Johns, R (2005) *Using the law in social work*. Exeter: Learning Matters.

Jones, C, Ferguson, I, Lavalette, M and Penketh, L (2003/2007) Social work and social justice: a manifesto for a new engaged practice, reprinted in Lavalette, M and Ferguson, I (eds) (2007) *International social work and the radical tradition*. Birmingham: Venture Press.

Jordon, W (1982) *Helping in social work*. London: Routledge and Kegan Paul.

Keeley, B and Clarke, M (2003) *Consultation with carers. Good practice guide*. **www.carers.org/data/ files/consultation-9.pdf**

Killick, J and Allan, K (2002) *Communication and the care of people with dementia*. Buckingham: Open University.

Kirby, P, Lanyon, C, Cronin, K and Sinclair, R (2003a) *Building a culture of participation. Involving children and young people in policy, service planning, delivery and evaluation. Research report*. London: Department for Education and Skills.

Kirby, P, Lanyon, C, Cronin, K and Sinclair, R (2003b) *Building a culture of participation. Involving children and young people in policy, service planning, delivery and evaluation. Handbook*. London: Department for Education and Skills.

Kirwan, N, Aubrey, J and Moules, T (2004) *Children's Fund Essex: Evaluation of the non-use of services. Final Report*. Chelmsford/Cambridge: The Centre for Research in Health and Social Care, Institute of Social Care.

Lansdown, G (1994) Children's rights, in Mayall, B (ed.) *Children's childhoods. Observed and experienced*. London: Falmer Press.

Lansdown, G (2001) *Promoting children's participation in democratic decision-making*. Florence: UNICEF Innocenti Research Centre (Innocenti Insight, A 6).

Levin, E (2004) *Involving service users and carers in social work education*. Resource guide no. 2. **www.scie.org.uk/publications/resourceguides/rg02/files/rg02.pdf**

Lindow, V (1999) *Evaluation of the National User Involvement Project. Findings*. **www.jrf.org.uk/knowledge/findings/socialcare/scr129.asp**

Lindow, V and Morris, J (1995) *Service user involvement: synthesis of findings and experience in the field of community care*. York: Joseph Rowntree Foundation.

Marchant, R (2001) The assessment of children with complex needs, in Howarth, J (ed.) *The child's world. Assessing children in need*. London: Jessica Kingsley Publishers.

Marchant, R and Kirby, P (2004) The participation of young children, in Willow, C Marchant, R, Kirby, P and Neale, B *Young children's citizenship. Ideas into practice*. York: Joseph Rowntree Foundation.

Marsh, P and Fisher, M (1992) *Good intentions: developing partnership in social services*. York: Joseph Rowntree Foundation/Community Care.

Martin, G and Younger, D (2000) Anti-oppressive practice: a route to the empowerment of people with dementia through communication and choice. *Journal of Psychiatric and Mental Health Nursing*, 7 (1), 59–67.

McDougall, T (1997) Patient empowerment: fact or fiction? *Mental Health Nursing*, 17 (1), 4–5.

Millington, P (2006) *Timeline of disability history*. **www.cdp.org.uk/documents/timeline/ timeline11.htm**

Molyneux, J and Irvine J (2004) Service user and carer involvement in social work training: a long and winding road? *Social Work Education*, 23 (3), 293–308.

Morgan, R (2006) *About social workers. A children's views report*. **www.rights4me.org/ content/beheardreports/3/about_social_workers_report.pdf**

Morris, J (1993) *Independent lives? Community care and disabled people*. London: Macmillan.

Morris, J (1994) *The shape of things to come? User-led social services*. Social Services policy forum paper no.3. London: National Institute of Social Work.

Morris, J (1998) The personal social services: Identifying the problem, in O'Neil, A and Statham, D (eds) *Shaping futures: Rights, welfare and personal social services*. London: NISW/Joseph Rowntree Foundation.

Murphy, J, Tester, S, Hubbard, G, Downs, M, and MacDonald, C (2005) Enabling frail older people with a communication difficulty to express their views: the use of Talking Mats™ as an interview tool. *Health and Social Care in the Community*, 13 (2), 95–107.

National Evaluation of the Children's Fund (NECF) (2005) *The Evaluator's Cookbook. Participatory evaluation exercises. A resource book for work with children and young people*. **www.ne-cf.org/core_files/ Binder2.pdf**

Nicholls, V, Wright, S, Waters, R and Wells, S (2003) *Surviving user-led research: reflections on supporting user-led research projects*. London: Mental Health Foundation.

Nocon, A and Qureshi, H (1998) *Outcomes of community care for users and carers. A social services perspective*. Buckingham: Open University Press.

Nolan, M, Grant, G, and Keady, J (1996) *Understanding family care. A multi-dimensional model of caring and coping*. Buckingham: Open University Press.

Northern Ireland Social Care Council (2002) *Codes of practice for social care workers and employers of social care workers*. Belfast: Northern Ireland Social Care Council.

Oldfield, C and Fowler, C (2004) *Mapping children and young people's participation in England*. **www.dfes.gov.uk/research/data/uploadfiles/RR584.pdf**

Oliver, M (1990) *The politics of disablement*. London: Macmillan.

Parker, J (2005) *Effective practice learning in social work*. Exeter: Learning Matters.

Prime Minister's Strategy Unit, Department for Work and Pensions, Department of Health, Department for Education and Skills and the Office of the Deputy Prime Minister (2005) *Improving the life chances of disabled people*. **www.strategy.gov.uk/downloads/work_areas/disability/disability_report/pdf/disability.pdf**

Princess Royal Trust for Carers (2005) *Who is a carer?* **www.carers.org/who-is-a-carer,118,GP.html**

Ramon, S and Anghel, R (2005) *Involving service users and carers in social work education at APU. Evaluation report*. Cambridge: Institute of Health and Social Care, Anglia Ruskin University (formerly Anglia Polytechnic University).

Research in Practice (2005) *TEAMWISE Using research evidence: A practical guide for teams*. **www.rip.org.uk/publication/handbooks.asp**

Rethink (2002) *The early years. National Schizophrenia Fellowship*. **www.rethink.org/about_rethink/the_early_years.html**

Rimmer, A and Harwood, K (2004) Citizen participation in the education of social workers. *Social Work Education*, 23 (3), 309–323.

Roberts, A (2006) *Mental health history timeline*. **www.mdx.ac.uk/www/study/ mhhtim.htm**

Robson, P, Begum, N and Locke, M (2003) *Developing user involvement: Working towards user-centred practice in voluntary organisations*. Bristol: The Policy Press.

Rose, D, Fleischman, P, Tonkiss, F, Campbell, P and Wykes, T (2003) *User and carer involvement in change management in a mental health context: Review of the literature. Report to the National Co-ordinating Centre for NHS Service Delivery and Organisation Research and Development (NCCSDO)*. **www.sdo.lshtm.ac.uk/files/project/17-final-report.pdf**

Ross, K (1995) Speaking in tongues: Involving users in day care services. *British Journal of Social Work*, 25 (6), 791–804.

Roulstone, A, Hudson, V, Kearney, J and Martin, A, with Warren, J (2006) *Working together: Carer participation in England, Wales and Northern Ireland*. Position paper 5. **www.scie.org.uk/publications/positionpapers/pp05.pdf**

Sainsbury Centre for Mental Health (SCMH) (2002) *Breaking the circles of fear. A review of the relationship between mental health services and African and Caribbean communities*. London: Sainsbury Centre for Mental Health.

Sartori, A (2003) User involvement in service planning, in Beresford, P, Fully engaged. *Community Care*, 13–19 November 2003. **www.communitycare.co.uk**

Scottish Executive (2004) *Protecting children and young people: Framework for standards*. **www.scotland.gov.uk/publications/2004/03/19102/34603**

Scottish Social Services Council (2005) *Code of practice for social service workers and employers*. Dundee: Scottish Social Services Council.

Shaping Our Lives National User Network (SOL) (2003) *What do we mean by 'service user' and 'user controlled' organisation?* **www.shapingourlives/service%20user%20definition.htm**

Shardlow, S and Nelson, P (2005) *Introducing social work*. Lyme Regis: Russell House Publishing.

Shephard, C and Treseder, P (2002) *Participation – spice it up!: Practical tools for engaging children and young people in planning and consultations*. Cardiff: Save the Children.

Simons, K (1995) *'I'm not complaining, but...': Complaints procedures in social services departments*. York: Joseph Rowntree Foundation in association with Community Care.

Simons, K (1999) *A place at the table? Involving people with learning difficulties in purchasing and commissioning services*. Kidderminster: British Institute of Learning Disabilities.

Sinclair, R and Franklin, A (2000) *Young people's participation. Quality Protects research briefing 3*. **www.rip.org.uk/publications/documents/QPB/QPRB3.asp**

Singh, B (2005) *Improving support for black disabled people: Lessons from community organisations on making change happen*. York: Joseph Rowntree Foundation.

Sketchley, L and Walker, R (2001) *Young people's charter of participation*. London: The Children's Society.

Small, N and Rhodes, P (2001) *Too ill to talk? User involvement and palliative care*. London: Routledge.

Stalker, K (2003) *Reconceptualising work with 'carers': New directions for policy and practice*. London: Jessica Kingsley Publishing.

Starkey, F (2003) The 'empowerment debate': consumerist, professional and liberation perspectives in health and social care. *Social Policy and Society*, 2 (4), 273–284.

Stewart, G (2006) *Key dates in the history of mental health and community care, the National Association of Mental Health, Mind Information Unit factsheet*. **www.mind.org.uk/Information/Factsheets/ History+of+mental+health/Key+Dates+in+the+History+of+Mental+Health+and+Community +Care.htm.**

Tew, J, Gell, C, and Foster, S (2004) *Learning from experience*. York: Higher Education Academy, NIMHE, West Midlands, Trent Workforce Development Confederation. **www.mhhe.heacademy.ac.uk/docs**

Thompson, N (1996) *People skills. A guide to effective practice in the human services*. Basingstoke: Macmillan.

Thornton, P (2000) *Older people speaking out: developing opportunities for influence*. York: York Publishing Service in association with Joseph Rowntree Foundation.

Together Working for Wellbeing (2006) *The Story of Together*. **www.together-uk.org**

Turner, M and Beresford, P (2005) *User controlled research. Its meanings and potential*. **www.shapingourlives.org.uk/Downloads/Usercontrolledresearch%20report.pdf**

Turner, M and Shaping Our Lives National User Network (2002) *Involving service users in social work education: Principles of best practice involvement*. **www.swap.ac.uk/ learning/usersw2.asp**

UK Advocacy Network (UKAN) (2007) *History of UKAN*. **www.u-kan.co.uk**

UK Disabled People's Council (2006) *Welcome to the United Kingdom Disabled People's Council (UKDPC)*. **www.bcodp.org.uk**

Voluntary Action Westminster (2006) *Involving people: A practical guide*. **www.vawcvs.org/ uploads/involving_people_a_practical_guide.pdf**

Waine, B, Tunstill, J and Meadows, P with Peel, T. (2005) *Developing social care: values and principles.* **www.scie.org.uk/publications/positionpapers/pp04/values.pdf**

Webb, R and Tossell, D (1991) *Social issues for carers. A community care perspective.* London: Edward Arnold.

Welsh Assembly Government (2004) *Stronger in partnership: Involving service users and carers in the design, delivery and evaluation of mental health services in Wales. Policy implementation guidance.* **www.wales.gov.uk/subihealth/content/keypubs/pdf/ stronger-partnership-e.pdf**

Williams, P (2006) *Social work with people with learning difficulties.* Exeter: Learning Matters.

Williams, V (2003) *Has anything changed? User involvement in promoting change and enhancing the quality of services for people with learning difficulties.* Bristol: Norah Fry Research Centre, University of Bristol.

Wistow, G (2005) *Developing social care: the past, the present and the future.* Position paper 4. **www.scie.org.uk/publications/positionpapers/pp04.pdf**

Wright, P, Turner, C, Clay, D and Mills, H (2006) *The participation of children and young people in developing social care.* Practice participation guide 6. **www.scie.org.uk/publications/practiceguides/ practiceguide06/files/pg06.pdf**

Youll, PJ and McCourt-Perrin, C (1993) *Raising voices: ensuring quality in residential care. An evaluation of the caring in homes initiative.* London: HMSO.

Young, A, Ackerman, J and Kyle, J (1998) *Looking on: Deaf people and the organisations of services.* Bristol: The Policy Press.

Young Independent People Presenting Educational Entertainment (YIPPEE) and Citizens as Trainers (CATS) (2002) How to consult with people who use services (or anyone else, for that matter), in CATS and YIPPEE *How to involve service users.* Salford: YIPPEE and CATS, University of Salford.

Index

adult users 80–95
  see also child users
  approaches 88–95
  background 85
  building/sustaining participation 81–8
  collective/public decision-making 91–3
  formal approaches 94
  individual decision-making 89–91
  legislation/policy 37–8 *Tables*
  organisational infrastructure 81–2
  positive relationships 82–3
  and social workers 67–9
  support mechanisms 84–8
advocacy 86
African Caribbean carers/users 87–8
Allan, K 89–90
Arnstein's model 50
arts media 87–8

barriers 52–7
Begum, N 82
benchmark statement x
benefits 4–5
Beresford, P 8, 84
Braye, S 19, 22, 23, 24, 48

carer involvement
  benefits of 24–6
  communication problems 53, 55
  definition 8–10
  and diversity 10
  emergence of movements 35–6, 119
    Appendix
  importance 22–4
  origins of interest 33–4
  and perceptions of social workers 67–9
  perceptions/experiences 54, 55–6
  values *see* value-base
Carr, S 21, 57
Carter, T 84
child users 98–116

see also adult users
  approaches to 110–11
  background 98–9
  group level participation 113–14
  high profile cases 99
  and human development 102
  involvement 100–6
  legislation/policy 37–8, 39–40 *Tables*
  levels of participation 111 *Fig.*
  marginalisation 100 *Fig.*
  national level participation 114
  perceptions of 101, 101–4
  personal decisions 111–12
  rights agenda 99
  skills needed 106–10
  summary 115
  sustaining participation 104–6
Children Acts 1989 and 2004 71
Children Now Participation Charter 2006
  74–5
Clare, L 65–6
Code of Practice for Social Care Workers
  23, 72
collective decision-making 91–3
communication problems 53, 55
community Care Needs Assessment Project
  2001 88
conferences 14
consumerist approach 47–8
Cox, S 65–6
creative arts media 87–8

Danso, C 26
decision-making, individual 89–91
definitions 5–10
democratic approach 47–8
disabled movements 119 *Appendix*

empowerment 62–3, 76–7
Evans, C 15
Every Child Matters 71

facilitation 57–8
Fisher, M 15
Fowler, C 81

group level participation 113–14

Hart, RA 50
Heron, C 87
historical perspective 32–3, 44, 119
    Appendix
holistic involvement 50–1
human development 101–2

individual decision-making 89–91
institutional structures/practices 54, 56
involvement
    approaches 47–8, 88–9
    barriers 52–6
    children 99–106
    facilitation 57–8
    holistic model 50–1
    levels 48–52
Irvine, J 10

Killick, J 89–90
Kirby, P 58, 59, 88, 91, 92, 101, 106, 110

legislation
    mandate 23–4
    and policy 37–43
Levin, E 71, 83
Lindow, V 87
Locke, M 82

mainstream lecturing 18
Marchant, R 101, 106, 110
marginalised groups 19–22
mental health survivors' movements 119
    Appendix
module revision 18
Molyneux, J 10

Nelson, P 109
networks 14–15

Oldfield, C 81
opportunities 10–22
    marginalised groups 19–22
    research/service evaluation 15–17

staff/student training 17–19
strategic planning/service development
    12–14
user-led services 14–15
user/carer involvement 11–12
organisational infrastructure 81–2
organisational resistance 55

participation 117
    elements 59
    empowerment 62–3, 77–8
    historical perspective 32–3, 44, 119
        Appendix
    involvement culture 47, 58–9
    key questions 3–4, 28
    ladders of 50
personal attendants 85
policy
    and legislation 37–43
    mandate 23–4
positive relationships 82–3
professional attitudes 53, 55, 63–6
professional development xii
professional mandates 23–4
programme management committee 18
project structure 18
public decision-making 91–3

reflective practice xii
relationships 82–3
relief care 85
research, participation 15–16
Robson, P 82
Rooots 87
Ross, K 86

Sartori, A 12
service development 12–15
service evaluation 15–16
service user *see* user
Shardlow, S 109
social work education ix–x
social workers, characteristics 67–9
strategic planning 12–15
student
    admissions 17
    assessment 18
support mechanisms 84–8

Thompson, N 63
time shortages 54, 56
tokenism 66

UN Convention on the Rights of the Child
     99
user involvement 11
  benefits of participation 25, 26–7
  communication problems 53, 55
  definition 7–8
  diversity of 10
  emergence of movements 35–6, 119
       Appendix
  importance of 22–4
  mandates 24
  origins of interest 33–4
  and perceptions of social workers 67–9
  perceptions/experiences 54, 55–6

user-led services 15–16
values *see* value-base

value-base 70
  core values 73–4
  influences on 70–2
  and practice 73–7
  tensions 73

Waine, B 70
Williams, P 86
Wright, P 59

Young peoples' charter of participation
     75–6
*Young people's skill development training
     manuel* 75